ESL Grades

Contents

Introduction

The *ESL Standards for Pre-K–12 Students* notes that "what is most important for ESOL learners is to function effectively in English and through English while learning challenging academic content." (p. 6) The Steck-Vaughn *ESL* series was designed to meet the needs of both second-language learners and teachers in achieving this goal.

To help ESOL students, the lessons in *ESL*:
• introduce concepts in context.
• highlight specific words or concepts with bold print and rebus clues.
• reinforce the skill with practice.

To help the teacher, the lessons in *ESL*:
• target grade-appropriate concepts.
• offer step-by-step instruction on beginning, intermediate, and advanced levels.
• build background knowledge.
• suggest ideas or words to be shared in the student's native language.
• signal when a phonics skill is unfamiliar to speakers of a specific language.
• point out idioms and multiple-meaning words that could cause confusion.
• suggest extension activities that apply the skill in a real-world situation.

THE ESOL STUDENT

Like all students, second-language learners bring to the classroom a wide variety of experiences, history, and culture. It is important to help these students feel appreciated and respected in the classroom. They have a wealth of knowledge that is interesting and beneficial to all students. By asking them to share stories and experiences about their native country as well as expressions and words in their native language, you will help them feel productive and successful.

 The multicultural icon in the lessons indicates ways for students to share aspects of their language and culture with the class.

 The whirling letter icon indicates multiple-meaning words that may confuse students.

ESOL students have different proficiency levels of the English language. Three levels are generally recognized.

Beginning: Students at this level have little or no understanding of the English language. They respond to questions and commands nonverbally by pointing or drawing. Some students at this level may give single word responses. They depend on nonprint clues to decode information in texts. To facilitate learning for beginning language learners, ask questions to which students can gesture to answer or respond with a "yes" or "no." Instruction should be slow, directed, and repetitive.

Intermediate: Intermediate ESOL students have a fundamental grasp of English. They understand and can use basic vocabulary associated with routine situations and needs. These students can respond using simple sentences, but their grammar is inconsistent. To read text, these language learners must have prior knowledge of the concepts. To facilitate learning for intermediate language learners, ask questions to which students can reply with words or short phrases. Instruction should be directed at first to make sure students understand the directions, and the page should be read to insure they know the content. It is also helpful to pair students.

Advanced: Students at this level are able to understand and communicate using English in most routine situations. They may need explanations of idioms, multiple-meaning words, and abstract concepts. They are often fluent readers and writers of English. Instruction for these learners includes responding to higher-level questions, reading the directions, and explaining words and phrases that might be confusing.

ORGANIZATION OF *ESL*

The *ESL* book is divided into four units.

Readiness: This section reinforces the basic skills students will need in the classroom and many real-world situations. There are two parts to each lesson. Part A introduces the skill or concept with picture clues and bold print to help second-language learners focus on the important words. Part B offers practice in a real-life application.

Alphabet Letters: This unit introduces the letters and their sounds. Each lesson has three sections. Part A introduces the letter, its sound, and its formation. Picture clues reinforce bold print words to further develop letter/sound recognition. Part B reinforces the words and sounds from Part A. In Part C, students apply the skill.

Numbers: The numbers unit introduces the numerals, number names, and quantity for numbers 1 to 10. It also offers instruction in three parts: introduction, reinforcement, and application.

Vocabulary: The vocabulary unit highlights basic words and background knowledge students need to function on a daily level or to understand topics taught in other curriculum areas. Like the readiness unit, two-part lessons first introduce the concept and then give practice applying it.

SPECIAL FEATURES

Individual Student Chart: The Individual Student Chart found on page 3 can help you track each student's skill understanding and progress.

Lessons: Each lesson in Units 2, 3, and 4 is a two-page spread. The left page is the model for teaching the pupil activity sheet found on the right page. The teacher model explains how to focus on the skill or ways to build background knowledge. Most importantly, the teacher model suggests the steps for teaching the page at each proficiency level.

Certificates: The two certificates on page 122 can be copied and distributed to students. One recognizes the student's efforts, and the other commends the student for successfully attaining a skill.

Take-Home Book: Beginning on page 123, you will find a take-home book about the American flag. Copies can be distributed to students. You may wish to read aloud the booklet several times before sending it home with students.

Individual Student Chart

Name _____

Skill	Accomplished (yes/no)	Date Page Completed
Unit 1: Readiness		
Lines		
More Lines		
Circles		
In		
Out		
Above		
Below		
Big and Little		
Up and Down		
Top, Middle, Bottom		
Same		
Different		
Missing Parts		
Groups		
First, Next, and Last		
Left and Right		
A Name		
An Address		
A Telephone Number		
Directions		
More Directions		
Unit 2: Alphabet Letters		
Letter a		
Letter b		
Letter c		
Letter d		
Letter e		
Letter f		
Letter g		
Letter h		
Letter i		
Letter j		
Letter k		
Letter l		
Letter m		
Letter n		

Skill	Accomplished (yes/no)	Date Page Completed
Letter o		
Letter p		
Letter q		
Letter r		
Letter s		
Letter t		
Letter u		
Letter v		
Letter w		
Letter x		
Letter y		
Letter z		
ABC order		
Unit 3: Numbers		
Number 1		
Number 2		
Number 3		
Number 4		
Number 5		
Number 6		
Number 7		
Number 8		
Number 9		
Number 10		
Numbers 1 to 10		
Unit 4: Vocabulary		
Clothes		
Colors		
Face Words		
Food		
House		
Pets		
Shapes		
Signs		
Ways to Move		
Weather		

Sample Readiness Lesson

The following lesson can be used as a model for teaching the activity pages in the Readiness unit.

PREPARATION

Preview Part A on the activity page. Duplicate the picture/item shown, either by drawing the item on the board, displaying a magazine picture, or better yet, showing the actual item. Children will need to become familiar with these items before learning concepts. Moreover, it is very important that they actively participate in the learning by moving something or by pantomiming. It will help them better understand the vocabulary and concept.

INTRODUCTION

Display the item and say a short, simple sentence about the concept as it relates to the item. Have children repeat the sentence. Introduce all the vocabulary and encourage children to actively participate as they repeat the words. Write the words on the board.

Beginning

Part A: Distribute the page. Direct children to look at the picture. Read the words or sentence aloud and have children repeat the words as they point to the picture. Ask questions about the picture to which children can respond with a nonverbal response or a yes/no answer.

Part B: Explain what children will do in Part B. Have them point to the first picture or word. Identify the picture name or word for children to repeat. Direct children through each step to find and write the answer. Again, if possible, have children actively participate in the process. Repeat with each picture or word.

Intermediate

Part A: Distribute the page. Direct children to look at the picture. Read the words or sentence aloud and have children repeat. Ask questions about the picture to which children can choose one of two answers or the answer can be found in a visual clue.

Part B: Explain what children will do in Part B. Have them point to the first picture or word. Identify the picture name or word for children to repeat. Ask questions that help children find and write the answer. After modeling how to do the work, read each remaining problem, but pause for children to find and write the answer on their own.

Advanced

Part A: Distribute the page. Direct children to look at the picture. Read the sentence aloud and have children repeat it. Invite children to talk about the picture. Encourage vocabulary development and practice as children talk.

Part B: Read aloud the directions. Ask children to skim the page to see if they have a question about any of the words or pictures. Have children complete the page independently.

Lines

A. Look at the picture and word.

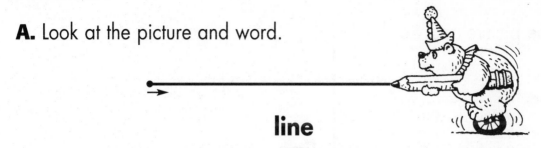

line

B. Put your pencil on each dot. Trace the lines.

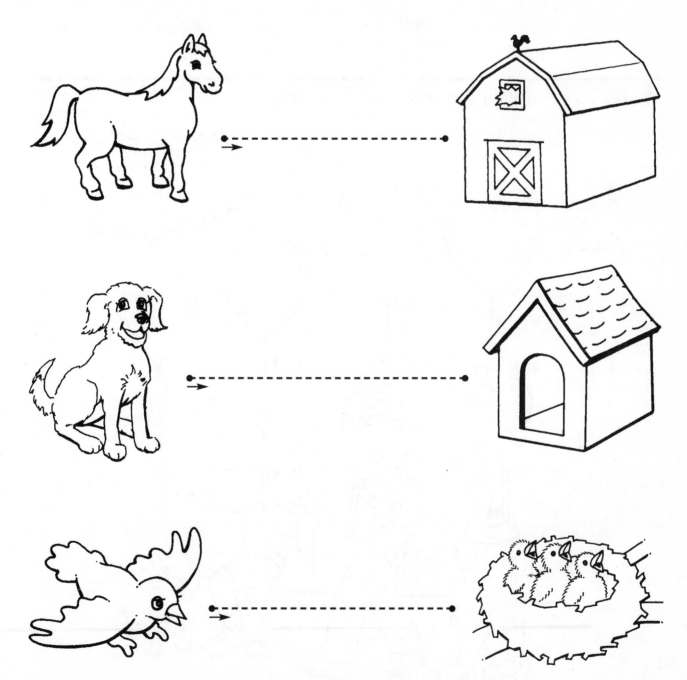

More Lines

A. Look at the picture and word.

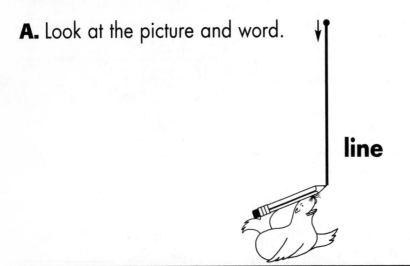

line

B. Put your pencil on each dot. Trace the lines.

Circles

A. Look at the picture and word.

circle

B. Put your pencil on each dot. Trace the circles.

In

A. Look at the picture and word.

in

B. Color each child that is in a car.

Out

A. Look at the picture and word.

out

B. Color each child that is out of the shoe.

Above

A. Look at the picture and word.

above

B. Color the bugs above the bird.

Below

A. Look at the picture and word.

below

B. Cut out the pictures. Paste the animals that live below the ship in the boxes.

Big and Little

A. Look at the picture and words.

big  **little**

B. Draw lines to match each animal with its home.

1.

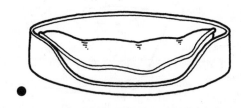

2.

Up and Down

A. Look at the picture and words.

___

B. Circle the animal that is up. Mark an **X** on the animal that is down.

1.

___

2.

Top, Middle, and Bottom

A. Look at the pictures and words.

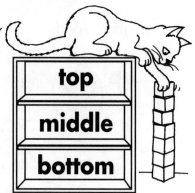

B. Color the top chair [red].

Color the middle chair [blue].

Color the bottom chair [green].

Same

A. Look at the pictures and word.

 **same**

B. Color the toys that are the same.

Different

A. Look at the pictures and word.

 different

B. Color the bowl in each set that is different.

1.

2.

 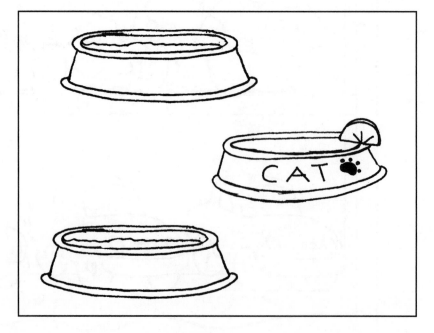

Missing Parts

A. Look at the pictures and sentence.

The wheels are **missing**.

B. Draw each missing part.

1.

2.

Groups

A. Look at the pictures and sentence.

  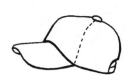

The chick goes with the **group**.

B. Circle the picture that goes with each group.

1.

2.

First, Next, and Last

A. Look at the pictures and words.

first   **next**   **last**

B. Circle what happened first. Cross out what happened next. Draw a box around what happened last.

1.

2.

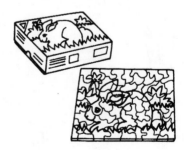

Left and Right

A. Look at the picture and words.

left   right

B. Cut out the pictures. Paste the animals in the balloons on the left.
Paste the toys in the balloons on the right.

A Name

A. Look at the picture. Listen to the sentences.

My **name** is Marco.

The **name** of my friend is Rob.

B. Write your name on the T-shirt. Then, color the shirt. Work with a friend to complete the sentence.

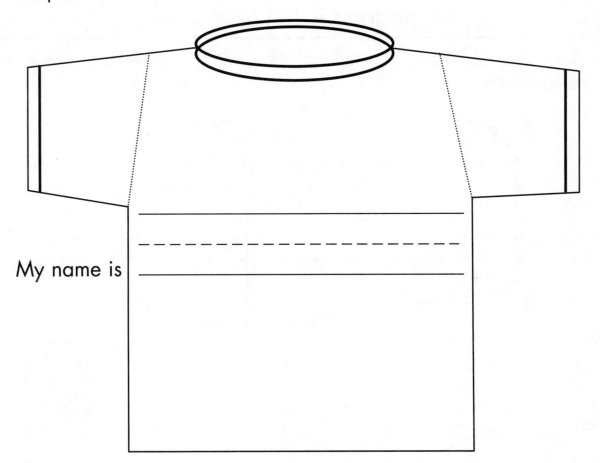

My name is

The name of my friend is _____.

Name _____ Date _____

An Address

A. Look at the picture. Listen to the sentence.

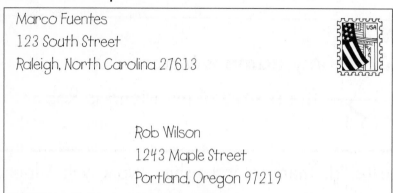

Marco Fuentes
123 South Street
Raleigh, North Carolina 27613

Rob Wilson
1243 Maple Street
Portland, Oregon 97219

My **address** is 123 South Street.

B. Write your address on the mailbox. Work with a partner to complete the envelope.

A Telephone Number

A. Look at the picture. Listen to the sentences.

My **telephone number** is 555-2468.

The **telephone number** for Rob is 555-9753.

B. Color the buttons that show your telephone number. Work with friends to complete the sentences.

My telephone number is _____.

The telephone number for _____ is

_____.

The telephone number for _____ is

_____.

Directions

A. Look at the pictures and words.

look   **listen**   **raise hand**   **say**

B. Look at each picture. Draw lines to match the word or words with the picture.

1.    **2.**

look   **listen**   **raise hand**   **say**

3.    **4.**

More Directions

A. Look at the pictures and words.

 circle   **underline**   write    color

B. Circle the .   Write your name on the .

Underline the .   Color the

Letter *a*

NOTE: Children whose native language is Italian may have problems with the short *a* sound.

INTRODUCTION

Display several apples. Hold up one apple and say: *This is an apple.* Have children repeat the sentence. Then, ask children what you have. Cut all the apples except one into slices and invite children to take a piece. As they take an apple, say: *(Name) has an apple.* Encourage children to repeat the sentence. Say *apple* again, stressing the beginning sound: /a/-/a/-/puhl/. Explain that /a/ is a sound for the letter *a* as children eat their snack.

 Invite children to share the word *apple* in their native language.

 Some children may confuse the short and long *a* sounds. They may hear *hate* instead of *hat*.

Beginning

Part A: Distribute page 27. Direct children to point to the first picture. Read the sentence aloud and have children repeat it. Pass a whole apple to each child and have the child repeat the sentence. Then, ask the following questions about the picture:
• *Who has the apple? Point to it.*
• *What does the cat have? Point to it.*
• *Does the cat have a ball?*
• *Does the cat have an apple?*
Repeat the sentence, stressing the *a* sound in each word: *The /k/-/a/-/t/ /h/-/a/-/a/-/z/ the /a/-/a/-/puhl/.* Tell children that *cat, has*, and *apple* all have the /a/ sound. Then, explain that the /a/ sound is at the beginning of the word *apple* and in the middle of the words *cat* and *has*. Point out that the words *cat* and *apple* are in dark print. Next, point out the capital and lowercase letters. Help children write *A* and *a*.

Part B: Tell children they will circle words that name pictures. Have children point to the apple and say the picture name. Then, have children point to the words in dark print in the sentence above. Ask questions that help children circle the word *apple*. Repeat with the picture of the cat. Remind children that the /a/ sound is at the beginning of the word *apple* and in the middle of the word *cat*.

Part C: Tell children they will color pictures whose names have the same /a/ sound as *apple*. Identify the picture of the hat. Have children repeat the word.

Say the picture name again, stressing the *a* sound: /h/-/a/-/a/-/t/. Tell children that *hat* has the /a/ sound and have them color the hat. Point out that the /a/ sound is in the middle of *hat*. Repeat the process with the remaining pictures.

Intermediate

Part A: Follow the directions in Part A of the Beginning section, but substitute these questions:
• *Who has the apple?*
• *What does the cat have?*

Part B: Tell children they will circle words that name pictures. Then, help children identify the pictures and words. Remind them that the /a/ sound is at the beginning of the word *apple* and in the middle of the word *cat*. Have them complete the section with a partner.

Part C: Tell children they will color pictures whose names have the same /a/ sound as *apple*. Identify the picture of the hat. Have children repeat the word. Say the picture name again, stressing the *a* sound: /h/-/a/-/a/-/t/. Tell children that *hat* has the /a/ sound and have them color the hat. Point out that the /a/ sound is in the middle of *hat*. Help children identify the names of the remaining pictures. Ask children to work with a partner to complete the page. As you review the answers, have children tell if they hear the /a/ sound at the beginning or in the middle of the picture names.

Advanced

Part A: Distribute page 27. Direct children to point to the first picture. Read the sentence aloud and have children repeat it. Invite children to talk about the picture. Repeat the sentence, stressing the *a* sound in each word: *The /k/-/a/-/a/-/t/ /h/-/a/-/a/-/z/ the /a/-/a/-/puhl/.* Tell children that *cat, has*, and *apple* all have the /a/ sound. Then, explain that the /a/ sound is at the beginning of the word *apple* and in the middle of the words *cat* and *has*. Point out that the words *cat* and *apple* are in dark print. Next, point out the capital and lowercase letters. Help children write *A* and *a*.

Parts B and C: Read aloud the directions and identify the pictures and words. Have children complete the page independently.

EXTENSION

Have children sit in a circle. Pass the apple to individual children. Say words that have the short *a* sound and challenge children to tell if the sound is at the beginning or in the middle of the word.

Letter *a*

A. Look at the picture. Listen to the sentence. Write the letters.

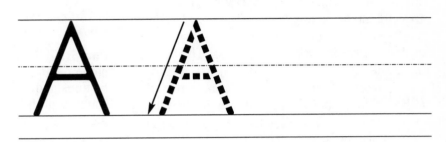

The **cat** has the **apple**.

B. Circle the word that matches the picture.

cat   **apple**   **cat**   apple

C. Color the pictures that have the same sound as **apple**.

Letter *b*

NOTE: Children whose native language is Chinese, Greek, Korean, and Spanish may have problems with the *b* sound.

INTRODUCTION

Take children to a school bus. Say: *This is a bus.* Have children repeat the sentence. Invite each child to board the bus and say: *(Name) gets on the bus.* Challenge children to repeat it. After all the children are sitting on the bus, say *bus* again, stressing the beginning sound: */b/-/b/-/us/.* Explain that /b/ is the sound for the letter *b*. Then, teach children the words to the song "The Wheels of the Bus."

 Group chairs in the classroom to role-play riding a bus. Invite children to share the word *bus* in their native language as they take a seat.

 Some children may confuse the sounds for the letters *b*, *p*, and *v*. They may hear *pea* or *v* instead of *bee*.

Beginning

Part A: Distribute page 29. Direct children to point to the first picture. Read the sentence aloud and have children repeat it. Invite each child to repeat the sentence individually. Then, ask the following questions about the picture:
• *Who gets on the bus? Point to it.*
• *What does the bee get on? Point to it.*
• *Is the bee in a boat?*
• *Is the bee on a bus?*

Repeat the sentence, stressing the *b* sound in each word: *The /b/-/b/-/ē/ gets on the /b/-/b/-/us/.* Tell children that *bee* and *bus* both have the /b/ sound. Then, explain that the /b/ sound is at the beginning of both words. Point out that the words *bee* and *bus* are in dark print. Next, point out the capital and lowercase letters. Help children write *B* and *b*.

Part B: Tell children they will circle words that name pictures. Have children point to the bus and say the picture name. Then, have children point to the words in dark print in the sentence above. Ask questions that help children circle the word *bus*. Repeat with the picture of the bee. Remind children that the /b/ sound is at the beginning of both words.

Part C: Tell children they will color pictures whose names have the same beginning sound as *bus*. Identify the picture of the bell. Have children repeat the word. Say the picture name again, stressing the *b* sound: */b/-/b/-/el/.* Tell children that *bell* has the *b* sound and have them color the bell. Point out that the /b/ sound is at the beginning of *bell*. Repeat the process with the remaining pictures.

Intermediate

Part A: Follow the directions in Part A of the Beginning section, but substitute these questions:
• *Who gets on the bus?*
• *What does the bee get on?*

Part B: Tell children they will circle words that name pictures. Then, help children identify the pictures and words. Remind them that the /b/ sound is at the beginning of both words. Have them complete the section with a partner.

Part C: Tell children they will color pictures whose names have the same beginning sound as *bus*. Identify the picture of the bell. Have children repeat the word. Say the picture name again, stressing the *b* sound: */b/-/b/-/el/.* Tell children that *bell* has the /b/ sound and have them color the picture. Point out that the /b/ sound is at the beginning of *bell*. Help children identify the names of the remaining pictures. Ask children to work with a partner to complete the page.

Advanced

Part A: Distribute page 29. Direct children to point to the picture of the bus in Part A. Read the sentence aloud and have children repeat it. Invite children to talk about the picture. Repeat the sentence, stressing the *b* sound in each word: *The /b/-/b/-/ē/ gets on the /b/-/b/-/us/.* Tell children that *bee* and *bus* both have the /b/ sound. Then, explain that the /b/ sound is at the beginning of both words. Point out that the words *bee* and *bus* are in dark print. Next, point out the capital and lowercase letters. Help children write *B* and *b*.

Parts B and C: Read aloud the directions and identify the pictures and words. Have children complete the page independently.

EXTENSION

Have children sit in a circle and display a bell. Remind children that *bell* begins with the *b* sound. Give the bell to one child. Say words and challenge the child to ring the bell when he or she hears a word that begins with the *b* sound. Continue passing the bell until each child has had a chance to play.

Letter *b*

A. Look at the picture. Listen to the sentence. Write the letters.

The **bee** gets on the **bus**.

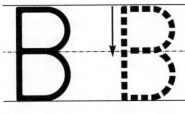

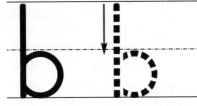

B. Circle the word that matches the picture.

bee   bus   **bee   bus**

C. Color the pictures that begin like **bus**.

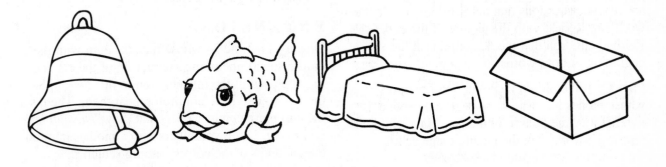

Letter c

NOTE: Children whose native language is Vietnamese may have problems with the hard *c* sound.

INTRODUCTION

Draw an outline of a cat on a sheet of butcher paper and display it. Say: *This is a cat*. Have children repeat the sentence. Next, display a cup. Say: *This is a cup*. Have children repeat the sentence. Then, say either the word *cat* or *cup* and invite individual children to point to the item and repeat the name. Say each word again, stressing the beginning sound: /k/-/k/-/at/ and /k/-/k/-/up/. Explain that /k/ is a sound for the letter *c*.

 Invite children to share the word *cat* in their native language and make the sound of a cat.

Beginning

Part A: Distribute page 31. Direct children to point to the picture of the cat with the cup in Part A. Read the sentence aloud and have children repeat it. Pass the cup to each child and have the child repeat the sentence. Then, ask the following questions about the picture:
• *Who has the cup? Point to it.*
• *What does the cat have? Point to it.*
• *Does the cat have a cup?*
• *Does the cat have a car?*

Repeat the sentence, stressing the hard *c* sound in each word: *The /k/-/k/-/at/ has a /k/-/k/-/up/*. Tell children that *cat* and *cup* both have the /k/ sound. Then, explain that the /k/ sound is at the beginning of both words. Point out that the words *cat* and *cup* are in dark print. Next, point out the capital and lowercase letters. Help children write *C* and *c*.

Part B: Tell children they will circle words that name pictures. Have children point to the cat and say the picture name. Then, have children point to the words in dark print in the sentence above. Ask questions that help children circle the word *cat*. Repeat with the picture of the cup. Remind children that the /k/ sound is at the beginning of both words.

Part C: Tell children they will color pictures whose names have the same beginning sound as *cat*. Identify the picture of the can. Have children repeat the word. Say the picture name again, stressing the hard *c* sound: /k/-/k/-/an/. Tell children that *can* has the /k/ sound and have them color the can. Point out that the /k/ sound is at the beginning of *can*. Repeat the process with the remaining pictures.

Intermediate

Part A: Follow the directions in Part A of the Beginning section, but substitute these questions:
• *Who has the cup?*
• *What does the cat have?*

Part B: Tell children they will circle words that name pictures. Then, help children identify the pictures and words. Remind them that the /k/ sound is at the beginning of both words. Have them complete the section with a partner.

Part C: Tell children they will color pictures whose names have the same beginning sound as *cat*. Identify the picture of the can. Have children repeat the word. Say the picture name again, stressing the hard *c* sound: /k/-/k/-/an/. Tell children that *can* has the /k/ sound and have them color the picture. Point out that the /k/ sound is at the beginning of *can*. Help children identify the names of the remaining pictures. Ask children to work with a partner to complete the page.

Advanced

Part A: Distribute page 31. Direct children to point to the picture of the cat with the cup in Part A. Read the sentence aloud and have children repeat it. Invite children to talk about the picture. Repeat the sentence, stressing the hard *c* sound in each word: *The /k/-/k/-/at/ has a /k/-/k/-/up/*. Tell children that *cat* and *cup* both have the /k/ sound. Then, explain that the /k/ sound is at the beginning of both words. Point out that the words *cat* and *cup* are in dark print. Next, point out the capital and lowercase letters. Help children write *C* and *c*.

Parts B and C: Read aloud the directions and identify the pictures and words. Have children complete the page independently.

EXTENSION

Display small items whose names begin with the hard *c* sound, including the picture of the cat and the cup used in the introduction to this lesson. Say the names and have children repeat them. Then, set the cup on the picture of the cat. Say: *The cup is on the cat*. Invite volunteers to set another item on the cat and say the corresponding sentence.

Letter *c*

A. Look at the picture. Listen to the sentence. Write the letters.

The **cat** has a **cup**.

C C C

c c

B. Circle the word that matches the picture.

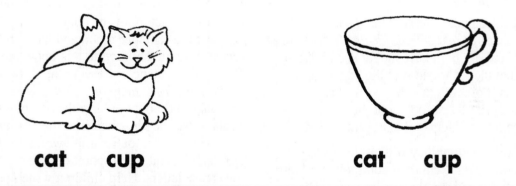

cat   cup   cat   cup

C. Color the pictures that begin like **cat**.

Letter *d*

NOTE: Children whose native language is Chinese, Greek, Spanish, or Urdu may have problems with the *d* sound.

INTRODUCTION

Take children outside and demonstrate how to use a shovel to dig. Using the tune for "The Farmer in the Dell," sing this sentence in a song innovation: *I can dig*. Then, invite each child to dig with the shovel and substitute the child's name in the song. Say *dig* again, stressing the beginning sound: */d/-/d/-/ig/*. Explain that /d/ is the sound for the letter *d*.

 Invite children to share the word *dig* in their native language.

Beginning

Part A: Distribute page 33. Direct children to point to the picture of the duck that can dig in Part A. Read the sentence aloud and have children repeat it. Pass the shovel to each child and have the child repeat the sentence. Then, ask the following questions about the picture:
• *Who can dig? Point to it.*
• *What can the duck do? Show me.*
• *Can the duck dig?*
• *Can the duck hop?*

Repeat the sentence, stressing the *d* sound in each word: *The /d/-/d/-/uk/ can /d/-/d/-/ig/*. Tell children that *duck* and *dig* both have the /d/ sound. Then, explain that the /d/ sound is at the beginning of both words. Point out that the words *duck* and *dig* are in dark print. Next, point out the capital and lowercase letters. Help children write *D* and *d*.

Part B: Tell children they will circle words that name pictures. Have children point to the picture that shows dig and say the picture name. Then, have children point to the words in dark print in the sentence above. Ask questions that help children circle the word *dig*. Repeat with the picture of the duck. Remind children that the /d/ sound is at the beginning of both words.

Part C: Tell children they will color pictures whose names have the same beginning sound as *dig*. Identify the picture of the doll. Have children repeat the word. Say the picture name again, stressing the *d* sound: */d/-/d/-/ol/*. Tell children that *doll* has the /d/ sound and have them color the doll.

Point out that the /d/ sound is at the beginning of *doll*. Repeat the process with the remaining pictures.

Intermediate

Part A: Follow the directions in Part A of the Beginning section, but substitute these questions:
• *Who can dig?*
• *What can the duck do?*

Part B: Tell children they will circle words that name pictures. Then, help children identify the pictures and words. Remind them that the /d/ sound is at the beginning of both words. Have them complete the section with a partner.

Part C: Tell children they will color pictures whose names have the same beginning sound as *dig*. Identify the picture of the doll. Have children repeat the word. Say the picture name again, stressing the *d* sound: */d/-/d/-/ol/*. Tell children that *doll* has the /d/ sound and have them color the picture. Point out that the /d/ sound is at the beginning of *doll*. Help children identify the names of the remaining pictures. Ask children to work with a partner to complete the page.

Advanced

Part A: Distribute page 33. Direct children to point to the picture of the duck that can dig in Part A. Read the sentence aloud and have children repeat it. Invite children to talk about the picture. Repeat the sentence, stressing the *d* sound in each word: *The /d/-/d/-/uk/ can /d/-/d/-/ig/*. Tell children that *duck* and *dig* both have the /d/ sound. Then, explain that the /d/ sound is at the beginning of both words. Point out that the words *duck* and *dig* are in dark print. Next, point out the capital and lowercase letters. Help children write *D* and *d*.

Parts B and C: Read aloud the directions and identify the pictures and words. Have children complete the page independently.

EXTENSION

Teach children the song "Five Little Ducks." Invite groups to role-play the song as they sing.

Letter *d*

A. Look at the picture. Listen to the sentence. Write the letters.

The **duck** can **dig**.

B. Circle the word that matches the picture.

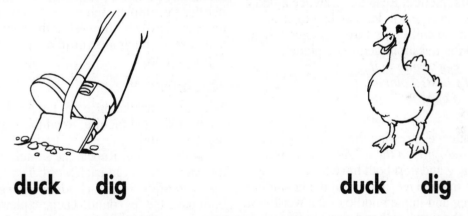

duck   dig   duck   dig

C. Color the pictures that begin like **dig**.

Letter *e*

NOTE: Students whose native language is Urdu may have problems with the short *e* sound.

INTRODUCTION

Display a hard boiled egg. Say: *This is an egg.* Have children repeat the sentence. Pass the egg to each child and have the child repeat the sentence. Then, take the children outside and divide them into two teams. Give each team an egg and a spoon. Explain that children will put the egg on the spoon and have a relay race. Challenge teams to quickly carry the egg to a specified point and return without dropping the egg. After returning to the classroom, break open one egg and let the children explore what it looks like on the inside. Say *egg* again, stressing the beginning sound: */e/-/e/-/g/*. Explain that /e/ is a sound for the letter *e*.

 Invite children to say the word *egg* in their native language.

 Some children may confuse the short *e* and *u* sounds. They may hear *ugh* instead of *egg*.

Beginning

Part A: Distribute page 35. Direct children to point to the first picture. Read the sentence aloud and have children repeat it. Pass an egg to each child and have the child repeat the sentence. Then, ask the following questions about the picture:
• *Where is the egg? Point to it.*
• *What is in the nest? Point to it.*
• *Is the egg in a cup?*
• *Is the egg in a nest?*

Repeat the sentence, stressing the *e* sound in each word: *The /e/-/e/-/g/ is in the /n/-/e/-/e/-/st/.* Tell children that *egg* and *nest* both have the /e/ sound. Then, explain that the /e/ sound is at the beginning of the word *egg* and in the middle of the word *nest*. Point out that the words *egg* and *nest* are in dark print. Next, point out the capital and lowercase letters. Help children write *E* and *e*.

Part B: Tell children they will circle words that name pictures. Have children point to the nest and say the picture name. Then, have children point to the words in dark print in the sentence above. Ask questions that help children circle the word *nest*. Repeat with the picture of the egg. Remind children that the /e/ sound is at the beginning of the word *egg* and in the middle of the word *nest*.

Part C: Tell children they will color pictures whose names have the have the same /e/ sound as *egg*. Identify the picture of the belt. Have children

repeat the word. Say the picture name again, stressing the *e* sound: */b/-/e/-/e/-/lt/*. Tell children that *belt* has the /e/ sound and have them color the belt. Point out that the /e/ sound is in the middle of *belt*. Repeat the process with the remaining pictures.

Intermediate

Part A: Follow the directions in Part A of the Beginning section, but substitute these questions:
• *Where is the egg?*
• *What is in the nest?*

Part B: Tell children they will circle words that name pictures. Then, help children identify the pictures and words. Remind them that the /e/ sound is at the beginning of the word *egg* and in the middle of the word *nest*. Have them complete the section with a partner.

Part C: Tell children they will color pictures whose names have the same /e/ sound as *egg*. Identify the picture of the belt. Have children repeat the word. Say the picture name again, stressing the *e* sound: */b/-/e/-/e/-/lt/*. Tell children that *belt* has the /e/ sound and have them color the belt. Point out that the /e/ sound is in the middle of *belt*. Help children identify the names of the remaining pictures. Ask children to work with a partner to complete the page. As you review the answers, have children tell if they hear the /e/ sound at the beginning or in the middle of the picture names.

Advanced

Part A: Distribute page 35. Direct children to point to the first picture. Read the sentence aloud and have children repeat it. Invite children to talk about the picture. Repeat the sentence, stressing the short *e* sound in each word: *The /e/-/e/-/g/ is in the /n/-/e/-/e/-/st/.* Tell children that *egg* and *nest* both have the /e/ sound. Then, explain that the /e/ sound is at the beginning of the word *egg* and in the middle of the word *nest*. Point out that the words *egg* and *nest* are in dark print. Next, point out the capital and lowercase letters. Help children write *E* and *e*.

Parts B and C: Read aloud the directions and identify the pictures and words. Have children complete the page independently.

EXTENSION

Tell children that *vest* has the /e/ sound in the middle. Then, help children make a vest from a large grocery sack. Challenge them to decorate it with pictures whose names have the /e/ sound.

Letter *e*

A. Look at the picture. Listen to the sentence. Write the letters.

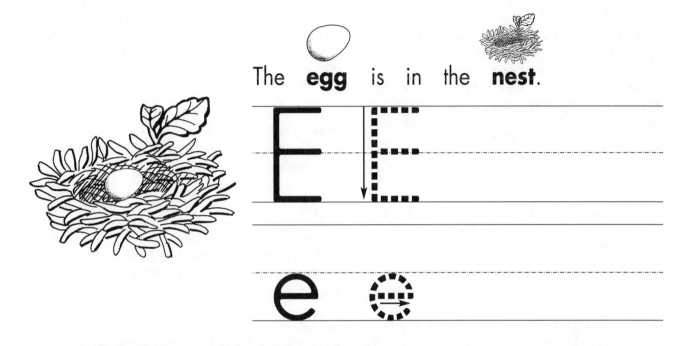

The **egg** is in the **nest**.

B. Circle the word that matches the picture.

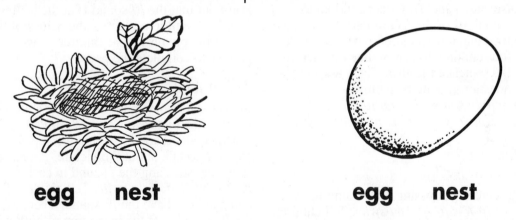

egg   nest   egg   nest

C. Color the pictures that have the same sound as **egg**.

EXIT

Letter *f*

NOTE: Children whose native language is Chinese, Japanese, or Urdu may have problems with the *f* sound.

INTRODUCTION

Make arrangements to visit a classroom that has a pet fish or draw a fish on paper. Say: *A fish can swim.* Have children repeat the sentence. Invite children to pantomime a swimming fish. Challenge each child to repeat the sentence individually as he or she swims like a fish. Say *fish* again, stressing the beginning sound: */f/-/f/-/ish/.* Explain that /f/ is the sound for the letter *f*.

 The homograph *fish* may confuse students. Explain that *fish* has two meanings. Pantomime the activity of fishing with a rod and then display a picture of a fish. Say simple sentences using the word in both ways and encourage students to pantomime the action or point to the fish to show the way the word is used. You might also like to explain that *fish* is both a singular and plural noun.

Beginning

Part A: Distribute page 37. Direct children to point to the pictures of the fish in Part A. Read the sentence aloud and have children repeat it. Invite groups of four children to pantomime the picture and chant the sentence together. Then, ask the following questions about the picture:
• *What animal do you see? Point to it.*
• *How many fish do you see? Point to each fish as I count.*
• *Do you see four fish?*
• *Do you see four feet?*

Repeat the sentence, stressing the *f* sound in each word: *The /f/-/f/-/ôr/ /f/-/f/-/ish/ swim.* Tell children that *four* and *fish* both have the /f/ sound. Then, explain that the /f/ sound is at the beginning of both words. Point out that the words *four* and *fish* are in dark print. Next, point out the capital and lowercase letters. Help children write *F* and *f*.

Part B: Tell children they will circle words that name pictures. Have children point to the fish and say the picture name. Then, have children point to the words in dark print in the sentence above. Ask questions that help children circle the word *fish*. Repeat with the picture of the four. Remind children that the /f/ sound is at the beginning of both words.

Part C: Tell children they will color pictures whose names have the same beginning sound as *fish*. Identify the picture of the feet. Have children repeat the word. Say the picture name again, stressing the *f* sound: */f/-/f/-/ēt/.* Tell children that *feet* has the *f* sound and have them color the feet. Point out that the /f/ sound is at the beginning of *feet*. Repeat the process with the remaining pictures.

Intermediate

Part A: Follow the directions in Part A of the Beginning section, but substitute these questions:
• *Do you see four or six fish?*
• *Do birds or fish swim?*

Part B: Tell children they will circle words that name pictures. Then, help children identify the pictures and words. Remind them that the /f/ sound is at the beginning of both words. Have them complete the section with a partner.

Part C: Tell children they will color pictures whose names have the same beginning sound as *fish*. Identify the picture of the feet. Have children repeat the word. Say the picture name again, stressing the *f* sound: */f/-/f/-/ēt/.* Tell children that *feet* has the *f* sound and have them color the feet. Point out that the /f/ sound is at the beginning of *feet*. Help children identify the names of the remaining pictures. Ask children to work with a partner to complete the page.

Advanced

Part A: Distribute page 37. Direct children to point to the pictures of the fish in Part A. Read the sentence aloud and have children repeat it. Invite children to talk about the picture. Repeat the sentence, stressing the *f* sound in each word: *The /f/-/f/-/ôr/ /f/-/f/-/ish/ swim.* Tell children that *four* and *fish* both have the /f/ sound. Then, explain that the /f/ sound is at the beginning of both words. Point out that the words *four* and *fish* are in dark print. Next, point out the capital and lowercase letters. Help children write *F* and *f*.

Parts B and C: Read aloud the directions and identify the pictures and words. Have children complete the page independently.

EXTENSION

Tell children that *feather* begins with the /f/ sound. Then, invite children to paint with feathers. Encourage them to include the letters *F* and *f* on their papers.

Letter *f*

A. Look at the picture. Listen to the sentence. Write the letters.

The **four** **fish** swim.

B. Circle the word that matches the picture.

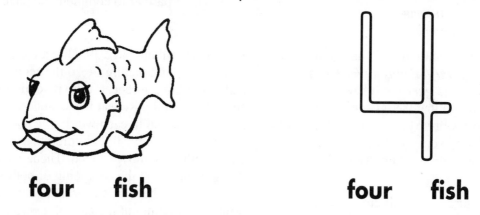

four   fish   four   fish

C. Color the pictures that begin like **fish**.

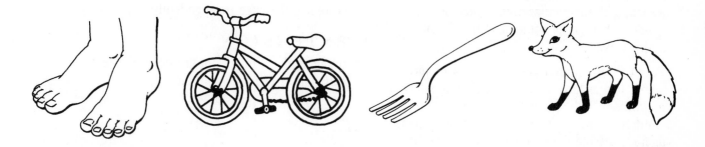

Letter *g*

NOTE: Children whose native language is Chinese or Greek may have problems with the hard *g* sound.

INTRODUCTION

Draw an outline of a goat on the board. Say: *This is a goat*. Have students repeat the sentence. Then, explain to students that you are going to tell a story about three goats. Ask them to raise their hand each time they hear the word *goat*. Then, slowly tell the story of *The Three Billy Goats Gruff* as you act it out. After the story, say *goat*, stressing the beginning sound: /g/-/g/-/ōt/. Explain that /g/ is the sound for the letter *g*.

 Invite children to say the word *goat* in their native language.

Beginning

Part A: Distribute page 39. Direct children to point to the first picture. Read the sentence aloud and have children repeat it. Invite each child to repeat the sentence individually. Then, ask the following questions about the picture:
• *Who is playing a game? Point to it.*
• *What is the goat playing? Point to it.*
• *Is the goat playing a game?*
• *Is a fish playing a game?*

Repeat the sentence, stressing the hard *g* sound in each word: *The /g/-/g/-/ōt/ plays a /g/-/g/-/ām/.* Tell children that *goat* and *game* both have the /g/ sound. Then, explain that the /g/ sound is at the beginning of both words. Point out that the words *goat* and *game* are in dark print. Next, point out the capital and lowercase letters. Help children write *G* and *g*.

Part B: Tell children they will circle words that name pictures. Have children point to the goat and say the picture name. Then, have children point to the words in dark print in the sentence above. Ask questions that help children circle the word *goat*. Repeat with the picture of the game. Remind children that the /g/ sound is at the beginning of both words.

Part C: Tell children they will color pictures whose names have the same beginning sound as *goat*. Identify the picture of the gum. Have children repeat the word. Say the picture name again, stressing the hard *g* sound: /g/-/g/-/um/.

Tell children that *gum* has the /g/ sound and have them color the gum. Point out that the /g/ sound is at the beginning of *gum*. Repeat the process with the remaining pictures.

Intermediate

Part A: Follow the directions in Part A of the Beginning section, but substitute these questions:
• *Is a goat or a fish playing a game?*
• *Is the goat playing a game or a gate?*

Part B: Tell children they will circle words that name pictures. Then, help children identify the pictures and words. Remind them that the /g/ sound is at the beginning of both words. Have them complete the section with a partner.

Part C: Tell children they will color pictures whose names have the same beginning sound as *goat*. Identify the picture of the gum. Have children repeat the word. Say the picture name again, stressing the hard *g* sound: /g/-/g/-/um/. Tell children that *gum* has the /g/ sound and have them color the gum. Point out that the /g/ sound is at the beginning of *gum*. Help children identify the names of the remaining pictures. Ask children to work with a partner to complete the page.

Advanced

Part A: Distribute page 39. Direct children to point to the first picture. Read the sentence aloud and have children repeat it. Invite children to talk about the picture. Repeat the sentence, stressing the hard *g* sound in each word: *The /g/-/g/-/ōt/ plays a /g/-/g/-/ām/.* Tell children that *goat* and *game* both have the /g/ sound. Then, explain that the /g/ sound is at the beginning of both words. Point out that the words *goat* and *game* are in dark print. Next, point out the capital and lowercase letters. Help children write *G* and *g*.

Parts B and C: Read aloud the directions and identify the pictures and words. Have children complete the page independently.

EXTENSION

Invite students to act out the story of *The Three Billy Goats Gruff* as you retell it.

Letter *g*

A. Look at the picture. Listen to the sentence. Write the letters.

The **goat** plays a **game**.

G G G

g g

B. Circle the word that matches the picture.

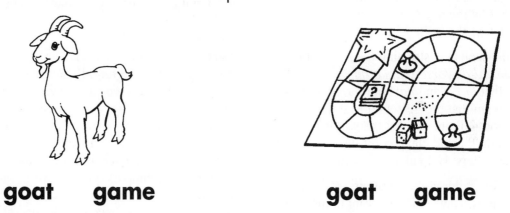

goat   game   goat   game

C. Color the pictures that begin like **goat**.

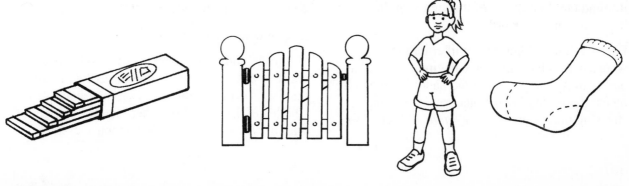

Letter *h*

NOTE: Children whose native language is French, Italian, Japanese, or Spanish may have problems with the *h* sound.

INTRODUCTION

Prefold newspaper to make a triangular hat for each child. Place a hat on your head and say: *I have a hat*. Have children repeat the sentence. Then, pass out a hat to each child and say: *(Name) has a hat*. Encourage children to repeat it. After all the children have a hat, say *hat* again, stressing the beginning sound: */h/-/h/-/at/*. Explain that /h/ is the sound for the letter *h*.

 Invite children to say the word *hat* in their native language and to describe or draw a hat that might be worn in their country.

Beginning

Part A: Distribute page 41. Direct children to point to the first picture. Read the sentence aloud and have children repeat it. Invite each child to repeat the sentence individually. Then, ask the following questions about the picture:
• *Who wears a hat? Point to it.*
• *What does the horse wear? Point to it.*
• *Is the hat on the dog?*
• *Is the hat on the horse?*

Repeat the sentence, stressing the *h* sound in each word: *The /h/-/h/-/ôrs/ wears a /h/-/h/-/at/*. Tell children that *horse* and *hat* both have the /h/ sound. Then, explain that the /h/ sound is at the beginning of both words. Point out that the words *horse* and *hat* are in dark print. Next, point out the capital and lowercase letters. Help children write *H* and *h*.

Part B: Tell children they will circle words that name pictures. Have children point to the horse and say the picture name. Then, have children point to the words in dark print in the sentence above. Ask questions that help children circle the word *horse*. Repeat with the picture of the hat. Remind children that the /h/ sound is at the beginning of both words.

Part C: Tell children they will color pictures whose names have the same beginning sound as *hat*. Identify the picture of the hand. Have children repeat the word. Say the picture name again, stressing the *h* sound: */h/-/h/-/and/*. Tell children

that *hand* has the *h* sound and have them color the hand. Point out that the /h/ sound is at the beginning of *hand*. Repeat the process with the remaining pictures.

Intermediate

Part A: Follow the directions in Part A of the Beginning section, but substitute these questions:
• *Who wears a hat?*
• *What does the horse wear?*

Part B: Tell children they will circle words that name pictures. Then, help children identify the pictures and words. Remind them that the /h/ sound is at the beginning of both words. Have them complete the section with a partner.

Part C: Tell children they will color pictures whose names have the same beginning sound as *hat*. Identify the picture of the hand. Have children repeat the word. Say the picture name again, stressing the *h* sound: */h/-/h/-/and/*. Tell children that *hand* has the *h* sound and have them color the hand. Point out that the /h/ sound is at the beginning of *hand*. Help children identify the names of the remaining pictures. Ask children to work with a partner to complete the page.

Advanced

Part A: Distribute page 41. Direct children to point to the first picture. Read the sentence aloud and have children repeat it. Invite children to talk about the picture. Repeat the sentence, stressing the *h* sound in each word: *The /h/-/h/-/ôrs/ wears a /h/-/h/-/at/*. Tell children that *horse* and *hat* both have the /h/ sound. Then, explain that the /h/ sound is at the beginning of both words. Point out that the words *horse* and *hat* are in dark print. Next, point out the capital and lowercase letters. Help children write *H* and *h*.

Parts B and C: Read aloud the directions and identify the pictures and words. Have children complete the page independently.

EXTENSION

Duplicate additional copies of page 41. Invite children to color, cut out, and paste the pictures that begin with the /h/ sound on their hats. Challenge them to draw other pictures that begin with the *h* sound to include on their hats.

Letter *h*

A. Look at the picture. Listen to the sentence. Write the letters.

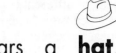 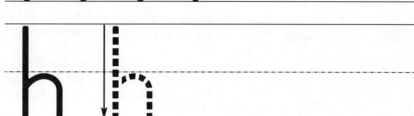

The **horse** wears a **hat**.

B. Circle the word that matches the picture.

horse   **hat**

horse   **hat**

C. Color the pictures that begin like **hat**.

Letter *i*

NOTE: Students whose native language is Greek, Italian, or Japanese may have problems with the short *i* sound.

INTRODUCTION

Display several ink pens of different colors. As you draw a picture with one pen, say: *I can draw with ink.* Have children repeat the sentence. Invite each child to choose a pen to draw with as the child repeats the sentence individually. Say *ink*, stressing the beginning sound: */i/-/i/-/nk/.* Explain that /i/ is a sound for the letter *i*.

 Invite children to draw a picture in ink of a special place in their native country. Invite children to tell why the place is special.

 Some children may confuse the short *i* and long *e* sounds. They may hear *meat* instead of *mitt*.

Beginning

Part A: Distribute page 43. Direct children to point to the first picture. Read the sentence aloud and have children repeat it. Pass an ink pen to each child and have the child repeat the sentence. Then, ask the following questions about the picture:
• *Who draws with ink? Point to it.*
• *What does the chick draw with? Point to it.*
• *Does the fish draw with ink?*
• *Does the chick draw with ink?*

Repeat the sentence, stressing the *i* sound in each word: *The /ch/-/i/-/i/-/k/ draws with /i/-/i/-/nk/.* Tell children that *chick*, *with*, and *ink* all have the /i/ sound. Then, explain that the /i/ sound is at the beginning of the word *ink* and in the middle of the words *chick* and *with*. Point out that the words *chick* and *ink* are in dark print. Next, point out the capital and lowercase letters. Help children write *I* and *i*.

Part B: Tell children they will circle words that name pictures. Have children point to the ink and say the picture name. Then, have children point to the words in dark print in the sentence above. Ask questions that help children circle the word *ink*. Repeat with the picture of the chick. Remind children that the /i/ sound is at the beginning of the word *ink* and in the middle of the word *chick*.

Part C: Tell children they will color pictures whose names have the have the same /i/ sound as *ink*. Identify the picture of the pig. Have children repeat the word. Say the picture name again, stressing the *i* sound: */p/-/i/-/i/-/g/.* Tell children that *pig* has the /i/ sound and have them color the

pig. Point out that the /i/ sound is in the middle of *pig*. Repeat the process with the remaining pictures.

Intermediate

Part A: Follow the directions in Part A of the Beginning section, but substitute these questions:
• *Who draws with ink?*
• *What does the chick draw with?*

Part B: Tell children they will circle words that name pictures. Then, help children identify the pictures and words. Remind them that the /i/ sound is at the beginning of the word *ink* and in the middle of the word *chick*. Have them complete the section with a partner.

Part C: Tell children they will color pictures whose names have the same /i/ sound as *ink*. Identify the picture of the pig. Have children repeat the word. Say the picture name again, stressing the *i* sound: */p/-/i/-/i/-/g/.* Tell children that *pig* has the /i/ sound and have them color the pig. Point out that the /i/ sound is in the middle of *pig*. Help children identify the names of the remaining pictures. Ask children to work with a partner to complete the page. As you review the answers, have children tell if they hear the /i/ sound at the beginning or in the middle of the picture names.

Advanced

Part A: Distribute page 43. Direct children to point to the first picture. Read the sentence aloud and have children repeat it. Invite children to talk about the picture. Repeat the sentence, stressing the *i* sound in each word: *The /ch/-/i/-/i/-/k/ draws with /i/-/i/-/nk/.* Tell children that *chick*, *with*, and *ink* all have the /i/ sound. Then, explain that the /i/ sound is at the beginning of the word *ink* and in the middle of the words *chick* and *with*. Point out that the words *chick* and *ink* are in dark print. Next, point out the capital and lowercase letters. Help children write *I* and *i*.

Parts B and C: Read aloud the directions and identify the pictures and words. Have children complete the page independently.

EXTENSION

Display a ruler and point out the inch marks. Tell children that *inch* begins with the letter *i*. Challenge partners to look for things that are one inch long. Have them record their answers by drawing with ink.

Letter *i*

A. Look at the picture. Listen to the sentence. Write the letters.

The **chick** draws with **ink**.

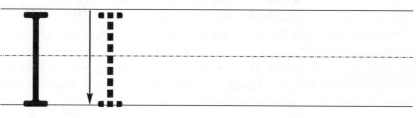

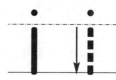

B. Circle the word that matches the picture.

chick   ink   **chick   ink**

C. Color the pictures that have the same sound as **ink**.

         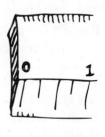

Letter *j*

NOTE: Children whose native language is Chinese, French, Greek, or Spanish may have problems with the *j* sound.

INTRODUCTION

Draw a picture of a candlestick. Then, teach children the rhyme "Jack Be Nimble." Invite children to jump over the candlestick as they chant the rhyme. After each child has had a chance to role-play Jack, say *jump*, stressing the beginning sound: */j/-/j/-/ump/*. Explain that /j/ is the sound for the letter *j*. Next, show children a plastic jar. Identify it and have children repeat the name. Help children understand that *jar* begins like *jump*. Repeat the activity, but have children substitute the jar for the candlestick in both the rhyme and the item over which to jump.

 Invite children to share the word *jump* in their native language.

 Some children may confuse the *j* and *ch* sounds. They may hear *chump* instead of *jump*.

Beginning

Part A: Distribute page 45. Direct children to point to the picture of the rabbit jumping in Part A. Read the sentence aloud and have children repeat it. Invite each child to repeat the sentence individually while jumping up and down. Then, ask the following questions about the picture:
• *What does Jack do? Show me.*
• *What does Jack jump over? Point to it.*
• *Is Jack running?*
• *Is Jack jumping over a jet?*

Repeat the sentence, stressing the *j* sound in each word: */j/-/j/-/ak/ /j/-/j/-/umps/* over a */j/-/j/-/âr/*. Tell children that *Jack, jumps,* and *jar* all have the /j/ sound. Then, explain that the /j/ sound is at the beginning of the words. Point out that the words *jumps* and *jar* are in dark print. Next, point out the capital and lowercase letters. Help children write *J* and *j*.

Part B: Tell children they will circle words that name pictures. Have children point to the jar and say the picture name. Then, have children point to the words in dark print in the sentence above. Ask questions that help children circle the word *jar*. Repeat with the picture for *jumps*. Remind children that the /j/ sound is at the beginning of both words.

Part C: Tell children they will color pictures whose names have the same beginning sound as *jumps*. Identify the picture of the jet. Have children repeat the word. Say the picture name again, stressing the *j* sound: */j/-/j/-/et/*. Tell children that *jet* has the *j* sound and have them color the jet. Point out that the /j/ sound is at the beginning of *jet*. Repeat the process with the remaining pictures.

Intermediate

Part A: Follow the directions in Part A of the Beginning section, but substitute these questions:
• *What does Jack do?*
• *What does Jack jump over?*

Part B: Tell children they will circle words that name pictures. Then, help children identify the pictures and words. Remind them that the /j/ sound is at the beginning of both words. Have them complete the section with a partner.

Part C: Tell children they will color pictures whose names have the same beginning sound as *jumps*. Identify the picture of the jet. Have children repeat the word. Say the picture name again, stressing the *j* sound: */j/-/j/-/et/*. Tell children that *jet* has the *j* sound and have them color the jet. Point out that the /j/ sound is at the beginning of *jet*. Help children identify the names of the remaining pictures. Ask children to work with a partner to complete the page.

Advanced

Part A: Distribute page 45. Direct children to point to the picture of the rabbit jumping in Part A. Read the sentence aloud and have children repeat it. Invite children to talk about the picture. Repeat the sentence, stressing the *j* sound in each word: */j/-/j/-/ak/ /j/-/j/-/umps/ over a /j/-/j/-/âr/*. Tell children that *Jack, jumps,* and *jar* all have the /j/ sound. Then, explain that the /j/ sound is at the beginning of the words. Point out that the words *jumps* and *jar* are in dark print. Next, point out the capital and lowercase letters. Help children write *J* and *j*.

Parts B and C: Read aloud the directions and identify the pictures and words. Have children complete the page independently.

EXTENSION

Provide jump ropes for children. Point out that *jump rope* begins with the letter *j*. Challenge children to use the jump rope to form the letter *j*. Then, invite children to jump rope.

Letter *j*

A. Look at the picture. Listen to the sentence. Write the letters.

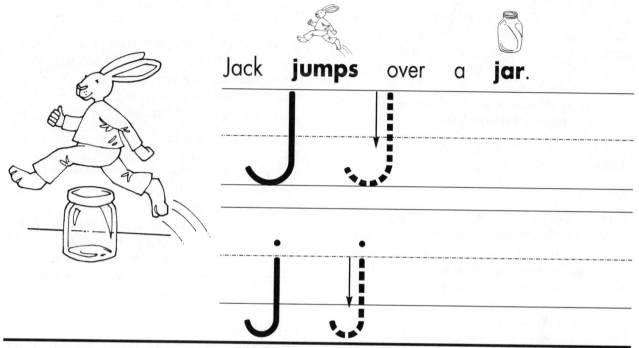

Jack **jumps** over a **jar**.

J J

j j

B. Circle the word that matches the picture.

jumps   **jar**   **jumps**   **jar**

C. Color the pictures that begin like **jumps**.

Letter *k*

NOTE: Children whose native language is Vietnamese may have problems with the *k* sound.

INTRODUCTION

Display a key and lock. Hold up the key and say: *This is a key*. Have children repeat the sentence. Invite children to use the key to open and close the lock. Say: *(Name) has a key*. Encourage children to repeat the sentence each time. Say *key* again, stressing the beginning sound: /k/-/k/-/ē/. Explain that /k/ is the sound for the letter *k*.

 Invite children to share the word *key* in their native language.

Beginning

Part A: Distribute page 47. Direct children to point to the first picture. Read the sentence aloud and have children repeat it. Invite each child to repeat the sentence individually. Then, ask the following questions about the picture:
• *Who has a key? Point to him.*
• *What does the king have? Point to it.*
• *Does the king have a carrot?*
• *Does the king have a key?*

Repeat the sentence, stressing the *k* sound in each word: *The /k/-/k/-/ing/ has a /k/-/k/-/ē/*. Tell children that *king* and *key* both have the /k/ sound. Then, explain that the /k/ sound is at the beginning of both words. Point out that the words *king* and *key* are in dark print. Next, point out the capital and lowercase letters. Help children write *K* and *k*.

Part B: Tell children they will circle words that name pictures. Have children point to the key and say the picture name. Then, have children point to the words in dark print in the sentence above. Ask questions that help children circle the word *key*. Repeat with the picture of the king. Remind children that the /k/ sound is at the beginning of both words.

Part C: Tell children they will color pictures whose names have the same beginning sound as *key*. Identify the picture of the kite. Have children repeat the word. Say the picture name again, stressing the *k* sound: /k/-/k/-/īt/. Tell children that *kite* has the *k* sound and have them color the kite. Point out that the /k/ sound is at the beginning of *kite*. Repeat the process with the remaining pictures.

Intermediate

Part A: Follow the directions in Part A of the Beginning section, but substitute these questions:
• *Does the king have a key or a carrot?*
• *Who has the key?*

Part B: Tell children they will circle words that name pictures. Then, help children identify the pictures and words. Remind them that the /k/ sound is at the beginning of both words. Have them complete the section with a partner.

Part C: Tell children they will color pictures whose names have the same beginning sound as *key*. Identify the picture of the kite. Have children repeat the word. Say the picture name again, stressing the *k* sound: /k/-/k/-/īt/. Tell children that *kite* has the *k* sound and have them color the kite. Point out that the /k/ sound is at the beginning of *kite*. Help children identify the names of the remaining pictures. Ask children to work with a partner to complete the page.

Advanced

Part A: Distribute page 47. Direct children to point to the first picture. Read the sentence aloud and have children repeat it. Invite children to talk about the picture. Repeat the sentence, stressing the *k* sound in each word: *The /k/-/k/-/ing/ has a /k/-/k/-/ē/*. Tell children that *king* and *key* both have the /k/ sound. Then, explain that the /k/ sound is at the beginning of both words. Point out that the words *king* and *key* are in dark print. Next, point out the capital and lowercase letters. Help children write *K* and *k*.

Parts B and C: Read aloud the directions and identify the pictures and words. Have children complete the page independently.

EXTENSION

Provide kite cutouts. Remind children that *kite* begins with the /k/ sound. Challenge children to draw a picture of something that begins like *kite* on their cutouts. Hang the kites from the ceiling using string.

Letter *k*

A. Look at the picture. Listen to the sentence. Write the letters.

The **king** has a **key**.

B. Circle the word that matches the picture.

king   **key**

king   **key**

C. Color the pictures that begin like **key**.

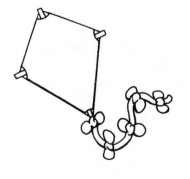   

Letter *l*

NOTE: Children whose native language is Chinese, Japanese, Korean, or Vietnamese may have problems with the *l* sound.

INTRODUCTION

Draw a lion on the board. Say: *This is a lion.* Have students repeat the sentence. Then, explain to students that you are going to tell a story about a lion and a mouse. Ask them to growl like a lion each time they hear the word *lion*. Then, slowly tell the story of *The Lion and the Mouse* as you act it out. After the story, say *lion*, stressing the beginning sound: /l/-/l/-/ī-uhn/. Explain that /l/ is the sound for the letter *l*.

 Invite children to say *lion* in their native language and share cultural celebrations in which they might see the symbol of a lion.

 Some children may confuse the *l* and *r* sounds. They may hear *ramp* instead of *lamp*.

Beginning

Part A: Distribute page 49. Direct children to point to the first picture. Read the sentence aloud and have children repeat it. Invite each child to repeat the sentence individually. Then, ask the following questions about the picture:
• *Who is reading? Point to it.*
• *What is the lion reading by? Point to it.*
• *Does the lion read beside a bed?*
• *Does the lion read beside a lamp?*

Repeat the sentence, stressing the *l* sound in each word: *The /l/-/l/-/ī-uhn/ reads by a /l/-/l/-/amp/.* Tell children that *lion* and *lamp* both have the /l/ sound. Then, explain that the /l/ sound is at the beginning of both words. Point out that the words *lion* and *lamp* are in dark print. Next, point out the capital and lowercase letters. Help children write *L* and *l*.

Part B: Tell children they will circle words that name pictures. Have children point to the lamp and say the picture name. Then, have children point to the words in dark print in the sentence above. Ask questions that help children circle the word *lamp*. Repeat with the picture of the lion. Remind children that the /l/ sound is at the beginning of both words.

Part C: Tell children they will color pictures whose names have the same beginning sound as *lion*. Identify the picture of the lake. Have children repeat the word. Say the picture name

again, stressing the *l* sound: /l/-/l/-/āk/. Tell children that *lake* has the *l* sound and have them color the lake. Point out that the /l/ sound is at the beginning of *lake*. Repeat the process with the remaining pictures.

Intermediate

Part A: Follow the directions in Part A of the Beginning section, but substitute these questions:
• *Who is reading?*
• *What is the lion reading by?*

Part B: Tell children they will circle words that name pictures. Then, help children identify the pictures and words. Remind them that the /l/ sound is at the beginning of both words. Have them complete the section with a partner.

Part C: Tell children they will color pictures whose names have the same beginning sound as *lion*. Identify the picture of the lake. Have children repeat the word. Say the picture name again, stressing the *l* sound: /l/-/l/-/āk/. Tell children that *lake* has the *l* sound and have them color the lake. Point out that the /l/ sound is at the beginning of *lake*. Help children identify the names of the remaining pictures. Ask children to work with a partner to complete the page.

Advanced

Part A: Distribute page 49. Direct children to point to the first picture. Read the sentence aloud and have children repeat it. Invite children to talk about the picture. Repeat the sentence, stressing the *l* sound in each word: *The /l/-/l/-/ī-uhn/ reads beside a /l/-/l/-/amp/.* Tell children that *lion* and *lamp* both have the /l/ sound. Then, explain that the /l/ sound is at the beginning of both words. Point out that the words *lion* and *lamp* are in dark print. Next, point out the capital and lowercase letters. Help children write *L* and *l*.

Parts B and C: Read aloud the directions and identify the pictures and words. Have children complete the page independently.

E X T E N S I O N

Draw a ladder outline on a long sheet of butcher paper. Between the rungs, draw pictures of words that begin with the letter *l*. Remind children that *ladder* begins with the letter *l*. Then, help them identify the pictures. Invite children to play ladder hopscotch. Demonstrate the game, saying the picture name before picking up the coin.

Letter *l*

A. Look at the picture. Listen to the sentence. Write the letters.

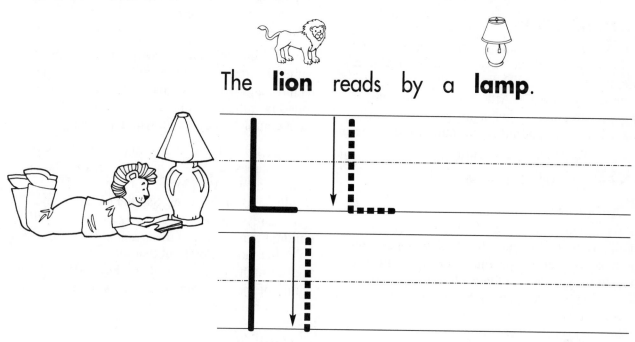

The **lion** reads by a **lamp**.

B. Circle the word that matches the picture.

lion   lamp

lion   lamp

C. Color the pictures that begin like **lion**.

49

Unit 2: Alphabet Letters
ESL K-1, SV 7096-3

Letter *m*

NOTE: Children whose native language is Chinese, Greek, or Spanish may have problems with the *m* sound.

INTRODUCTION

Draw a mouse on the board. Say: *This is a mouse.* Have children repeat the sentence. Teach children the rhyme "Hickory Dickory Dock." Invite them to role-play the mouse. After several recitations, say *mouse*, stressing the beginning sound: */m/-/m/-/ows/.* Explain that /m/ is the sound for the letter *m.*

 Invite children to share the word *mouse* in their native language.

Beginning

Part A: Distribute page 51. Direct children to point to the first picture. Read the sentence aloud and have children repeat it. Invite each child to repeat the sentence individually. Then, ask the following questions about the picture:
• *What does the mouse get? Point to it.*
• *Who gets milk? Point to it.*
• *Is the mouse getting juice?*
• *Is the mouse getting milk?*

Repeat the sentence, stressing the *m* sound in each word: *The /m/-/m/-/ows/ gets /m/-/m/-/ilk/.* Tell children that *mouse* and *milk* both have the /m/ sound. Then, explain that the /m/ sound is at the beginning of both words. Point out that the words *mouse* and *milk* are in dark print. Next, point out the capital and lowercase letters. Help children write *M* and *m.*

Part B: Tell children they will circle words that name pictures. Have children point to the milk and say the picture name. Then, have children point to the words in dark print in the sentence above. Ask questions that help children circle the word *milk.* Repeat with the picture of the mouse. Remind children that the /m/ sound is at the beginning of both words.

Part C: Tell children they will color pictures whose names have the same beginning sound as *mouse.* Identify the picture of the moon. Have children repeat the word. Say the picture name again, stressing the *m* sound: */m/-/m/-/o͞on/.* Tell children that *moon* has the *m* sound and have them color the moon. Point out that the /m/ sound is at the beginning of *moon.* Repeat the process with the remaining pictures.

Intermediate

Part A: Follow the directions in Part A of the Beginning section, but substitute these questions:
• *Is the mouse getting juice or milk?*
• *Who gets milk?*

Part B: Tell children they will circle words that name pictures. Then, help children identify the pictures and words. Remind them that the /m/ sound is at the beginning of both words. Have them complete the section with a partner.

Part C: Tell children they will color pictures whose names have the same beginning sound as *mouse.* Identify the picture of the moon. Have children repeat the word. Say the picture name again, stressing the *m* sound: */m/-/m/-/o͞on/.* Tell children that *moon* has the *m* sound and have them color the moon. Point out that the /m/ sound is at the beginning of *moon.* Help children identify the names of the remaining pictures. Ask children to work with a partner to complete the page.

Advanced

Part A: Distribute page 51. Direct children to point to the first picture. Read the sentence aloud and have children repeat it. Invite children to talk about the picture. Repeat the sentence, stressing the *m* sound in each word: *The /m/-/m/-/ows/ gets /m/-/m/-/ilk/.* Tell children that *mouse* and *milk* both have the /m/ sound. Then, explain that the /m/ sound is at the beginning of both words. Point out that the words *mouse* and *milk* are in dark print. Next, point out the capital and lowercase letters. Help children write *M* and *m.*

Parts B and C: Read aloud the directions and identify the pictures and words. Have children complete the page independently.

EXTENSION

Make a mouse mask out of a paper plate and construction paper. Display the mask and explain that *mouse* and *mask* both begin with the letter *m.* Invite children to make a mouse mask and pantomime "Hickory Dickory Dock."

Letter *m*

A. Look at the picture. Listen to the sentence. Write the letters.

 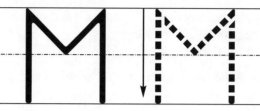

The **mouse** gets **milk**.

M M

m m

B. Circle the word that matches the picture.

mouse   milk

mouse   milk

C. Color the pictures that begin like **mouse**.

Letter *n*

NOTE: Children whose native language is Chinese, Greek, Spanish, or Urdu may have problems with the *n* sound.

INTRODUCTION

Make arrangements for the children to visit the school nurse. Ask the nurse to talk with the children about her job. After returning to the classroom, say: *(Nurse's name) is a nurse.* Have children repeat the sentence. Say *nurse* again, stressing the beginning sound: */n/-/n/-/ûrs/.* Explain that /n/ is the sound for the letter *n*.

 Invite children to say the word *nurse* in their native language.

Beginning

Part A: Distribute page 53. Direct children to point to the first picture. Read the sentence aloud and have children repeat it. Invite each child to repeat the sentence individually. Then, ask the following questions about the picture:
• *Who sees a nest? Point to it.*
• *What does the nurse see? Point to it.*
• *Does the nurse see a nest?*
• *Does the nurse see a nail?*

Repeat the sentence, stressing the *n* sound in each word: *The /n/-/n/-/ûrs/ sees a /n/-/n/-/est/.* Tell children that *nurse* and *nest* both have the /n/ sound. Then, explain that the /n/ sound is at the beginning of both words. Point out that the words *nurse* and *nest* are in dark print. Next, point out the capital and lowercase letters. Help children write *N* and *n*.

Part B: Tell children they will circle words that name pictures. Have children point to the nest and say the picture name. Then, have children point to the words in dark print in the sentence above. Ask questions that help children circle the word *nest*. Repeat with the picture of the nurse. Remind children that the /n/ sound is at the beginning of both words.

Part C: Tell children they will color pictures whose names have the same beginning sound as *nurse*. Identify the picture of the nail. Have children repeat the word. Say the picture name again, stressing the *n* sound: */n/-/n/-/āl/.* Tell children that *nail* has the *n* sound and have them color the nail. Point out that the /n/ sound is at the beginning of *nail*. Repeat the process with the remaining pictures.

Intermediate

Part A: Follow the directions in Part A of the Beginning section, but substitute these questions:
• *Does the nurse see a nail or a nest?*
• *Who sees the nest?*

Part B: Tell children they will circle words that name pictures. Then, help children identify the pictures and words. Remind them that the /n/ sound is at the beginning of both words. Have them complete the section with a partner.

Part C: Tell children they will color pictures whose names have the same beginning sound as *nurse*. Identify the picture of the nail. Have children repeat the word. Say the picture name again, stressing the *n* sound: */n/-/n/-/āl/.* Tell children that *nail* has the *n* sound and have them color the nail. Point out that the /n/ sound is at the beginning of *nail*. Help children identify the names of the remaining pictures. Ask children to work with a partner to complete the page.

Advanced

Part A: Distribute page 53. Direct children to point to the first picture. Read the sentence aloud and have children repeat it. Invite children to talk about the picture. Repeat the sentence, stressing the *n* sound in each word: *The /n/-/n/-/ûrs/ sees a /n/-/n/-/est/.* Tell children that *nurse* and *nest* both have the /n/ sound. Then, explain that the /n/ sound is at the beginning of both words. Point out that the words *nurse* and *nest* are in dark print. Next, point out the capital and lowercase letters. Help children write *N* and *n*.

Parts B and C: Read aloud the directions and identify the pictures and words. Have children complete the page independently.

EXTENSION

Display a newspaper and tell children that *newspaper* begins with the letter *n*. Challenge children to circle each capital and lowercase *n* they find in a newspaper ad or headline.

Letter *n*

A. Look at the picture. Listen to the sentence. Write the letters.

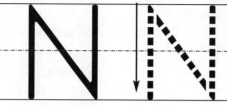

The **nurse** sees a **nest**.

N N N

n n

B. Circle the word that matches the picture.

nurse   **nest**

nurse   **nest**

C. Color the pictures that begin like **nurse**.

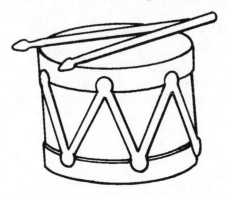

Letter o

INTRODUCTION

Display a jar of olives. Hold up one olive and say: *This is an olive.* Have children repeat the sentence. Then, ask children what you have. Invite each child to taste an olive and encourage the child to repeat the sentence. Say *olive* again, stressing the beginning sound: /o/-/o/-/liv/. Explain that /o/ is a sound for the letter *o* as children eat their snack.

 Invite children to share the word *olive* in their native language. Some children may be from countries where olives are an important crop. Encourage them to share information about how olives grow.

 Some children may confuse the short *o, u,* and *aw* sounds.

Beginning

Part A: Distribute page 55. Direct children to point to the first picture. Read the sentence aloud and have children repeat it. Pass the jar of olives to each child and have the child repeat the sentence. Then, ask the following questions about the picture:
• *Who is eating an olive? Point to it.*
• *What is the frog eating? Point to it.*
• *Is the frog eating bugs?*
• *Is the frog eating an olive?*

Repeat the sentence, stressing the *o* sound in each word: *The /fr/-/o/-/o/-/g/ eats an /o/-/o/-/liv/.* Tell children that *frog* and *olive* both have the /o/ sound. Then, explain that the /o/ sound is at the beginning of the word *olive* and in the middle of the word *frog.* Point out that the words *frog* and *olive* are in dark print. Next, point out the capital and lowercase letters. Help children write *O* and *o.*

Part B: Tell children they will circle words that name pictures. Have children point to the olive and say the picture name. Then, have children point to the words in dark print in the sentence above. Ask questions that help children circle the word *olive.* Repeat with the picture of the frog. Remind children that the /o/ sound is at the beginning of the word *olive* and in the middle of the word *frog.*

Part C: Tell children they will color pictures whose names have the have the same /o/ sound as *olive.* Identify the picture of the doll. Have children repeat the word. Say the picture name again, stressing the *o* sound: /d/-/o/-/o/-/l/. Tell children that *doll* has the /o/ sound and have them color the doll. Point out that the /o/ sound is in the middle of *doll.* Repeat the process with the remaining pictures.

Intermediate

Part A: Follow the directions in Part A of the Beginning section, but substitute these questions:
• *What is the frog eating?*
• *Who is eating an olive?*

Part B: Tell children they will circle words that name pictures. Then, help children identify the pictures and words. Remind them that the /o/ sound is at the beginning of the word *olive* and in the middle of the word *frog.* Have them complete the section with a partner.

Part C: Tell children they will color pictures whose names have the same /o/ sound as *olive.* Identify the picture of the doll. Have children repeat the word. Say the picture name again, stressing the *o* sound: /d/-/o/-/o/-/l/. Tell children that *doll* has the /o/ sound and have them color the doll. Point out that the /o/ sound is in the middle of *doll.* Help children identify the names of the remaining pictures. Ask children to work with a partner to complete the page. As you review the answers, have children tell if they hear the /o/ sound at the beginning or in the middle of the picture names.

Advanced

Part A: Distribute page 55. Direct children to point to the first picture. Read the sentence aloud and have children repeat it. Invite children to talk about the picture. Repeat the sentence, stressing the *o* sound in each word: *The /fr/-/o/-/o/-/g/ eats an /o/-/o/-/liv/.* Tell children that *frog* and *olive* both have the /o/ sound. Then, explain that the /o/ sound is at the beginning of the word *olive* and in the middle of the word *frog.* Point out that the words *frog* and *olive* are in dark print. Next, point out the capital and lowercase letters. Help children write *O* and *o.*

Part B and C: Read aloud the directions and identify the pictures and words. Have children complete the page independently.

EXTENSION

Display a large box. Remind children that *box* has the /o/ sound in the middle of the word. Then, challenge children to say a word that has the /o/ sound before tossing a ball into the box.

Letter o

A. Look at the picture. Listen to the sentence. Write the letters.

The **frog** eats an **olive**.

B. Circle the word that matches the picture.

frog   olive   frog   olive

C. Color the pictures that have the same sound as **olive**.

Letter *p*

NOTE: Children whose native language is Korean or Vietnamese may have problems with the *p* sound.

INTRODUCTION

Draw an outline of a pig on the board. Say: *This is a pig.* Have students repeat the sentence. Then, explain to students that you are going to tell a story about three pigs. Ask them to raise their hand each time they hear the word *pig*. Then, slowly tell the story of *The Three Little Pigs* as you act it. After the story, say *pig*, stressing the beginning sound: */p/-/p/-/ig/*. Explain that /p/ is the sound for the letter *p*.

 Invite children to say the word *pig* in their native language.

Beginning

Part A: Distribute page 57. Direct children to point to the first picture. Read the sentence aloud and have children repeat it. Invite each child to repeat the sentence individually. Then, ask the following questions about the picture:
• *What does the pig have? Point to it.*
• *Who has the pail? Point to it.*
• *Does the pig have a puppy?*
• *Does the pig have a pail?*

Repeat the sentence, stressing the *p* sound in each word: *The /p/-/p/-/ig/ has a /p/-/p/-/āl/.* Tell children that *pig* and *pail* both have the /p/ sound. Then, explain that the /p/ sound is at the beginning of both words. Point out that the words *pig* and *pail* are in dark print. Next, point out the capital and lowercase letters. Help children write *P* and *p*.

Part B: Tell children they will circle words that name pictures. Have children point to the pail and say the picture name. Then, have children point to the words in dark print in the sentence above. Ask questions that help children circle the word *pail*. Repeat with the picture of the pig. Remind children that the /p/ sound is at the beginning of both words.

Part C: Tell children they will color pictures whose names have the same beginning sound as *pig*. Identify the picture of the pin. Have children repeat the word. Say the picture name again, stressing the *p* sound: */p/-/p/-/in/*. Tell children that *pin* has the *p* sound and have them color the pin. Point out that the /p/ sound is at the beginning of *pin*. Repeat the process with the remaining pictures.

Intermediate

Part A: Follow the directions in Part A of the Beginning section, but substitute these questions:
• *Does the pig have a pail or a puppy?*
• *Who has the pail?*

Part B: Tell children they will circle words that name pictures. Then, help children identify the pictures and words. Remind them that the /p/ sound is at the beginning of both words. Have them complete the section with a partner.

Part C: Tell children they will color pictures whose names have the same beginning sound as *pig*. Identify the picture of the pin. Have children repeat the word. Say the picture name again, stressing the *p* sound: */p/-/p/-/in/*. Tell children that *pin* has the *p* sound and have them color the pin. Point out that the /p/ sound is at the beginning of *pin*. Help children identify the names of the remaining pictures. Ask children to work with a partner to complete the page.

Advanced

Part A: Distribute page 57. Direct children to point to the first picture. Read the sentence aloud and have children repeat it. Invite children to talk about the picture. Repeat the sentence, stressing the *p* sound in each word: *The /p/-/p/-/ig/ has a /p/-/p/-/āl/.* Tell children that *pig* and *pail* both have the /p/ sound. Then, explain that the /p/ sound is at the beginning of both words. Point out that the words *pig* and *pail* are in dark print. Next, point out the capital and lowercase letters. Help children write *P* and *p*.

Parts B and C: Read aloud the directions and identify the pictures and words. Have children complete the page independently.

EXTENSION

Invite students to act out the story of *The Three Little Pigs* as you retell it.

Letter *p*

A. Look at the picture. Listen to the sentence. Write the letters.

The **pig** has a **pail**.

B. Circle the word that matches the picture.

pig   pail

pig   pail

C. Color the pictures that begin like **pig**.

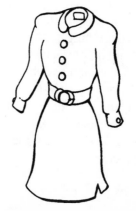

Unit 2: Alphabet Letters
ESL K-1, SV 7096-3

Letter q

INTRODUCTION

Display a quilt. Say: *This is a quilt*. Have children repeat the sentence. Invite children to sit on the quilt. Say: *(Name) sits on the quilt.* Encourage children to repeat the sentence each time. After all the children are sitting on the quilt, say *quilt* again, stressing the beginning sound: */kw/-/kw/-/ilt/.* Explain that /kw/ is the sound for the letter *q*. Discuss how people might use a quilt and have children describe the patterns they see.

 Invite children to share a word for a blanket in their native language.

Beginning

Part A: Distribute page 59. Direct children to point to the first picture. Read the sentence aloud and have children repeat it. Invite each child to repeat the sentence individually. Then, ask the following questions about the picture:
• *Who makes a quilt? Point to her.*
• *What is the queen making? Point to it.*
• *Is the queen making a pie?*
• *Is the queen making a quilt?*

Repeat the sentence, stressing the *q* sound in each word: *The /kw/-/kw/-/ēn/ makes a /kw/-/kw/-/ilt/.* Tell children that *queen* and *quilt* both have the /kw/ sound. Then, explain that the /kw/ sound is at the beginning of both words. Point out that the words *queen* and *quilt* are in dark print. Next, point out the capital and lowercase letters. Help children write *Q* and *q*.

Part B: Tell children they will circle words that name pictures. Have children point to the queen and say the picture name. Then, have children point to the words in dark print in the sentence above. Ask questions that help children circle the word *queen*. Repeat with the picture of the quilt. Remind children that the /kw/ sound is at the beginning of both words.

Part C: Tell children they will color pictures whose names have the same beginning sound as *quilt*. Identify the picture of the quarter. Have children repeat the word. Say the picture name again, stressing the *q* sound: */kw/-/kw/-/ôr-tûr/.* Tell children that *quarter* has the *q* sound and have them color the quarter. Point out that the /kw/ sound is at the beginning of *quarter*. Repeat the process with the remaining pictures.

Intermediate

Part A: Follow the directions in Part A of the Beginning section, but substitute these questions:
• *Does the queen make a quilt or a pie?*
• *Who makes a quilt?*

Part B: Tell children they will circle words that name pictures. Then, help children identify the pictures and words. Remind them that the /kw/ sound is at the beginning of both words. Have them complete the section with a partner.

Part C: Tell children they will color pictures whose names have the same beginning sound as *quilt*. Identify the picture of the quarter. Have children repeat the word. Say the picture name again, stressing the *q* sound: */kw/-/kw/-/ôr-tûr/.* Tell children that *quarter* has the *q* sound and have them color the quarter. Point out that the /kw/ sound is at the beginning of *quarter*. Help children identify the names of the remaining pictures. Ask children to work with a partner to complete the page.

Advanced

Part A: Distribute page 59. Direct children to point to the first picture. Read the sentence aloud and have children repeat it. Invite children to talk about the picture. Repeat the sentence, stressing the *q* sound in each word: *The /kw/-/kw/-/ēn/ makes a /kw/-/kw/-/ilt/.* Tell children that *queen* and *quilt* both have the /kw/ sound. Then, explain that the /kw/ sound is at the beginning of both words. Point out that the words *queen* and *quilt* are in dark print. Next, point out the capital and lowercase letters. Help children write *Q* and *q*.

Parts B and C: Read aloud the directions and identify the pictures and words. Have children complete the page independently.

EXTENSION

Invite children to help make a paper quilt. Give each child a square of construction paper. Challenge them to draw a picture whose name begins with the /kw/ sound. Paste the pictures together on a large sheet of butcher paper. You might ask children to sit on the quilt to listen to a story.

Letter *q*

A. Look at the picture. Listen to the sentence. Write the letters.

The **queen** makes a **quilt**.

B. Circle the word that matches the picture.

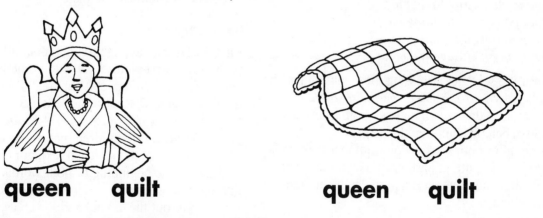

queen   **quilt**   **queen**   **quilt**

C. Color the pictures that begin like **quilt**.

Letter *r*

NOTE: Children whose native language is Greek, Japanese, Korean, Spanish, or Vietnamese may have problems with the *r* sound.

INTRODUCTION

Point to a rug and say: *This is a rug*. Have children repeat the sentence. Invite children to sit on the rug one at a time. Say: *(Name) sits on the rug*. Encourage children to repeat the sentence each time. After all the children are sitting on the rug, say *rug* again, stressing the beginning sound: /r/-/r/-/ug/. Explain that /r/ is the sound for the letter *r*.

 Invite children to share the word *rug* in their native language.

 Some children may confuse the *r* and *l* sounds. They may hear *lug* instead of *rug*.

Beginning

Part A: Distribute page 61. Direct children to point to the first picture. Read the sentence aloud and have children repeat it. Invite each child to repeat the sentence individually. Then, ask the following questions about the picture:
• *Who is on the rug? Point to it.*
• *What is the rabbit sitting on? Point to it.*
• *Is the rabbit sitting on the rug?*
• *Is the rabbit sitting on a chair?*

Repeat the sentence, stressing the *r* sound in each word: *The /r/-/r/-/ab-it/ sits on the /r/-/r/-/ug/.* Tell children that *rabbit* and *rug* both have the /r/ sound. Then, explain that the /r/ sound is at the beginning of both words. Point out that the words *rabbit* and *rug* are in dark print. Next, point out the capital and lowercase letters. Help children write *R* and *r*.

Part B: Tell children they will circle words that name pictures. Have children point to the rug and say the picture name. Then, have children point to the words in dark print in the sentence above. Ask questions that help children circle the word *rug*. Repeat with the picture of the rabbit. Remind children that the /r/ sound is at the beginning of both words.

Part C: Tell children they will color pictures whose names have the same beginning sound as *rug*. Identify the picture of the ring. Have children repeat the word. Say the picture name again, stressing the *r* sound: /r/-/r/-/ing/. Tell children

that *ring* has the *r* sound and have them color the ring. Point out that the /r/ sound is at the beginning of *ring*. Repeat the process with the remaining pictures.

Intermediate

Part A: Follow the directions in Part A of the Beginning section, but substitute these questions:
• *Is the rabbit on the rug or on the table?*
• *Is a rabbit or a frog on the rug?*

Part B: Tell children they will circle words that name pictures. Then, help children identify the pictures and words. Remind them that the /r/ sound is at the beginning of both words. Have them complete the section with a partner.

Part C: Tell children they will color pictures whose names have the same beginning sound as *rug*. Identify the picture of the ring. Have children repeat the word. Say the picture name again, stressing the *r* sound: /r/-/r/-/ing/. Tell children that *ring* has the *r* sound and have them color the ring. Point out that the /r/ sound is at the beginning of *ring*. Help children identify the names of the remaining pictures. Ask children to work with a partner to complete the page.

Advanced

Part A: Distribute page 61. Direct children to point to the first picture. Read the sentence aloud and have children repeat it. Invite children to talk about the picture. Repeat the sentence, stressing the *r* sound in each word: *The /r/-/r/-/ab-it/ sits on the /r/-/r/-/ug/.* Tell children that *rabbit* and *rug* both have the /r/ sound. Then, explain that the /r/ sound is at the beginning of both words. Point out that the words *rabbit* and *rug* are in dark print. Next, point out the capital and lowercase letters. Help children write *R* and *r*.

Parts B and C: Read aloud the directions and identify the pictures and words. Have children complete the page independently.

EXTENSION

Tell children that *rain* begins with the letter *r*. Then, pass out large tear-shaped raindrops. Invite students to draw a picture that begins like *rain* on the drop.

Letter *r*

A. Look at the picture. Listen to the sentence. Write the letters.

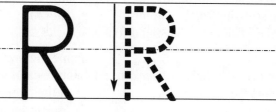

The **rabbit** sits on the **rug**.

R R

r r

B. Circle the word that matches the picture.

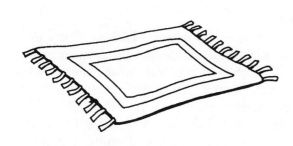

rabbit   **rug**   **rabbit**   **rug**

C. Color the pictures that begin like **rug**.

Letter *s*

NOTE: Children whose native language is Chinese, French, Greek, Japanese, Urdu, or Vietnamese may have problems with the *s* sound.

INTRODUCTION

Display several pairs of socks. Hold one sock up and say: *This is a sock.* Have children repeat the sentence. Invite each child to choose one sock, say the sentence individually, and then find the sock's match. Say *sock* again, stressing the beginning sound: */s/-/s/-/ok/*. Explain that /s/ is the sound for the letter *s*.

 Invite children to share the word *sock* in their native language.

 Some children may confuse the *s*, *z*, *sh*, and *th* sounds.

Beginning

Part A: Distribute page 63. Direct children to point to the first picture. Read the sentence aloud and have children repeat it. Invite each child to repeat the sentence individually. Then, ask the following questions about the picture:
• *What does the seal wash? Point to it.*
• *Who washes socks? Point to it.*
• *Does the seal wash a glass?*
• *Does the seal wash socks?*

Repeat the sentence, stressing the *s* sound in each word: *The /s/-/s/-/ēl/ washes /s/-/s/-/oks/.* Tell children that *seal* and *socks* both have the /s/ sound. Then, explain that the /s/ sound is at the beginning of both words. You may also wish to point out that the /s/ sound is at the end of *socks*, too. Point out that the words *seal* and *socks* are in dark print. Next, point out the capital and lowercase letters. Help children write *S* and *s*.

Part B: Tell children they will circle words that name pictures. Have children point to the seal and say the picture name. Then, have children point to the words in dark print in the sentence above. Ask questions that help children circle the word *seal*. Repeat with the picture of the socks. Remind children that the /s/ sound is at the beginning of both words.

Part C: Tell children they will color pictures whose names have the same beginning sound as *socks*. Identify the picture of the sun. Have children repeat the word. Say the picture name again, stressing the *s* sound: */s/-/s/-/un/.* Tell children that *sun* has the *s* sound and have them color the sun. Point out that the /s/ sound is at the beginning of *sun*. Repeat the process with the remaining pictures.

Intermediate

Part A: Follow the directions in Part A of the Beginning section, but substitute these questions:
• *Does a seal or a dog wash socks?*
• *Does the seal wash socks or a sun?*

Part B: Tell children they will circle words that name pictures. Then, help children identify the pictures and words. Remind them that the /s/ sound is at the beginning of both words. Have them complete the section with a partner.

Part C: Tell children they will color pictures whose names have the same beginning sound as *socks*. Identify the picture of the sun. Have children repeat the word. Say the picture name again, stressing the *s* sound: */s/-/s/-/un/.* Tell children that *sun* has the *s* sound and have them color the sun. Point out that the /s/ sound is at the beginning of *sun*. Help children identify the names of the remaining pictures. Ask children to work with a partner to complete the page.

Advanced

Part A: Distribute page 63. Direct children to point to the first picture. Read the sentence aloud and have children repeat it. Invite children to talk about the picture. Repeat the sentence, stressing the *s* sound in each word: *The /s/-/s/-/ēl/ washes /s/-/s/-/oks/.* Tell children that *seal* and *socks* both have the /s/ sound. Then, explain that the /s/ sound is at the beginning of both words. You may also wish to point out that the /s/ sound is at the end of *socks*, too. Point out that the words *seal* and *socks* are in dark print. Next, point out the capital and lowercase letters. Help children write *S* and *s*.

Parts B and C: Read aloud the directions and identify the pictures and words. Have children complete the page independently.

EXTENSION

Tell children that the word *six* begins with the letter *s*. Invite partners to find a group of six items, such as crayons or blocks, to share with the class.

Letter *s*

A. Look at the picture. Listen to the sentence. Write the letters.

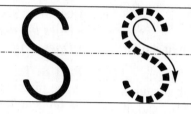

The **seal** washes **socks**.

B. Circle the word that matches the picture.

seal   socks

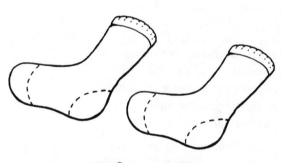

seal   socks

C. Color the pictures that begin like **socks**.

Letter *t*

NOTE: Children whose native language is Korean, Spanish, or Urdu may have problems with the *t* sound.

INTRODUCTION

Display a tie. Say: *This is a tie*. Have children repeat the sentence. Invite each child to put on the tie and say: *(Name) wears a tie*. Challenge children to repeat it. After all the children have worn the tie, say *tie* again, stressing the beginning sound: */t/-/t/-/ī/*. Explain that /t/ is the sound for the letter *t*.

 Invite children to say *tie* in their native language.

 Some children may confuse the *t* and *th* sounds. They may hear *thigh* instead of *tie*.

 The homograph *tie* may confuse students. Explain that *tie* has two meanings. Show children how to tie a knot with yarn or string. Then, display the tie. Say simple sentences using the word in both ways and encourage students to pantomime tying a knot or point to the tie to show the way the word is used.

Beginning

Part A: Distribute page 65. Direct children to point to the first picture. Read the sentence aloud and have children repeat it. Invite each child to repeat the sentence individually. Then, ask the following questions about the picture:
• *Who wears a tie? Point to it.*
• *What does the tiger wear? Point to it.*
• *Does the tiger wear tape?*
• *Does the tiger wear a tie?*

Repeat the sentence, stressing the *t* sound in each word: *The /t/-/t/-/ī-gûr/ wears a /t/-/t/-/ī/*. Tell children that *tiger* and *tie* both have the /t/ sound. Then, explain that the /t/ sound is at the beginning of both words. Point out that the words *tiger* and *tie* are in dark print. Next, point out the capital and lowercase letters. Help children write *T* and *t*.

Part B: Tell children they will circle words that name pictures. Have children point to the tiger and say the picture name. Then, have children point to the words in dark print in the sentence above. Ask questions that help children circle the word *tiger*. Repeat with the picture of the tie. Remind children that the /t/ sound is at the beginning of both words.

Part C: Tell children they will color pictures whose names have the same beginning sound as *tie*. Identify the picture of the tape. Have children

repeat the word. Say the picture name again, stressing the *t* sound: */t/-/t/-/āp/*. Tell children that *tape* has the *t* sound and have them color the tape. Point out that the /t/ sound is at the beginning of *tape*. Repeat the process with the remaining pictures.

Intermediate

Part A: Follow the directions in Part A of the Beginning section, but substitute these questions:
• *Does the tiger wear tape or a tie?*
• *Does a tiger or a turtle wear a tie?*

Part B: Tell children they will circle words that name pictures. Then, help children identify the pictures and words. Remind them that the /t/ sound is at the beginning of both words. Have them complete the section with a partner.

Part C: Tell children they will color pictures whose names have the same beginning sound as *tie*. Identify the picture of the tape. Have children repeat the word. Say the picture name again, stressing the *t* sound: */t/-/t/-/āp/*. Tell children that *tape* has the *t* sound and have them color the tape. Point out that the /t/ sound is at the beginning of *tape*. Help children identify the names of the remaining pictures. Ask children to work with a partner to complete the page.

Advanced

Part A: Distribute page 65. Direct children to point to the first picture. Read the sentence aloud and have children repeat it. Invite children to talk about the picture. Repeat the sentence, stressing the *t* sound in each word: *The /t/-/t/-/ī-gûr/ wears a /t/-/t/-/ī/*. Tell children that *tiger* and *tie* both have the /t/ sound. Then, explain that the /t/ sound is at the beginning of both words. Point out that the words *tiger* and *tie* are in dark print. Next, point out the capital and lowercase letters. Help children write *T* and *t*.

Parts B and C: Read aloud the directions and identify the pictures and words. Have children complete the page independently.

EXTENSION

Tell children that *table* also begins like *tie*. Then, spray a small amount of shaving cream on a table. Invite students to write *T* and *t* on the table.

Letter *t*

A. Look at the picture. Listen to the sentence. Write the letters.

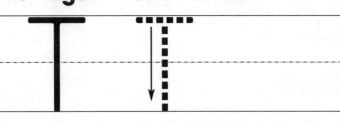

The **tiger** wears a **tie**.

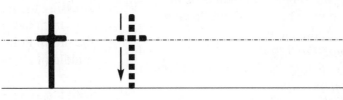

B. Circle the word that matches the picture.

tiger   tie

tiger   tie

C. Color the pictures that begin like **tie**.

Letter *u*

INTRODUCTION

Gather several balls. Toss one ball into the air and say: *The ball goes up*. Have children repeat the sentence. Then, invite children to toss balls into the air as they repeat the sentence. Say *up* again, stressing the beginning sound: */u/-/u/-/p/*. Explain that /u/ is a sound for the letter *u*.

 Invite children to share the word *up* in their native language. Encourage children to jump up each time.

Beginning

Part A: Distribute page 67. Direct children to look at the picture of the duck going up in Part A. Read the sentence aloud and have children repeat it. Invite each child to repeat the sentence individually and then jump up. Then, ask the following questions about the picture:
• *Who goes up? Point to it.*
• *Where does the duck go? Show me by jumping.*
• *Does the duck go down?*
• *Does the duck go up?*

Repeat the sentence, stressing the *u* sound in each word: *The /d/-/u/-/k/ goes /u/-/u/-/p/*. Tell children that *duck* and *up* both have the /u/ sound. Then, explain that the /u/ sound is at the beginning of the word *up* and in the middle of the word *duck*. Point out that the words *duck* and *up* are in dark print. Next, point out the capital and lowercase letters. Help children write *U* and *u*.

Part B: Tell children they will circle words that name pictures. Have children point to the duck and say the picture name. Then, have children point to the words in dark print in the sentence above. Ask questions that help children circle the word *duck*. Repeat with the picture showing up. Remind children that the /u/ sound is at the beginning of the word *up* and in the middle of the word *duck*.

Part C: Tell children they will color pictures whose names have the same /u/ sound as *up*. Identify the picture of the drum. Have children repeat the word. Say the picture name again, stressing the *u* sound: */dr/-/u/-/u/-/m/*. Tell children that *drum* has the /u/ sound and have them color the drum. Point out that the /u/ sound is in the middle of *drum*. Repeat the process with the remaining pictures.

Intermediate

Part A: Follow the directions in Part A of the Beginning section, but substitute these questions:
• *Does the duck or the cat go up?*
• *Who goes up?*

Part B: Tell children they will circle words that name pictures. Then, help children identify the pictures and words. Remind them that the /u/ sound is at the beginning of the word *up* and in the middle of the word *duck*. Have them complete the section with a partner.

Part C: Tell children they will color pictures whose names have the same /u/ sound as *up*. Identify the picture of the drum. Have children repeat the word. Say the picture name again, stressing the *u* sound: */dr/-/u/-/u/-/m/*. Tell children that *drum* has the /u/ sound and have them color the drum. Point out that the /u/ sound is in the middle of *drum*. Help children identify the names of the remaining pictures. Ask children to work with a partner to complete the page. As you review the answers, have children tell if they hear the /u/ sound at the beginning or in the middle of the picture names.

Advanced

Part A: Distribute page 67. Direct children to look at the picture of the duck going up in Part A. Read the sentence aloud and have children repeat it. Invite children to talk about the picture. Repeat the sentence, stressing the *u* sound in each word: *The /d/-/u/-/k/ goes /u/-/u/-/p/*. Tell children that *duck* and *up* both have the /u/ sound. Then, explain that the /u/ sound is at the beginning of the word *up* and in the middle of the word *duck*. Point out that the words *duck* and *up* are in dark print. Next, point out the capital and lowercase letters. Help children write *U* and *u*.

Parts B and C: Read aloud the directions and identify the pictures and words. Have children complete the page independently.

EXTENSION

Display an umbrella. Remind children that *umbrella* begins like *up*. Pass the umbrella to each child and invite the child to sit under it. Challenge children to say a word that begins with the /u/ sound while they are under the umbrella.

Letter *u*

A. Look at the picture. Listen to the sentence. Write the letters.

 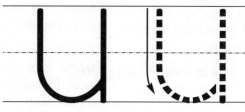

The **duck** goes **up**.

U U

u u

B. Circle the word that matches the picture.

duck   up

duck   up

C. Color the pictures that have the same sound as **up**.

  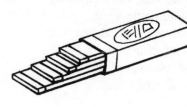 

Letter *v*

NOTE: Children whose native language is Chinese, Italian, Japanese, or Spanish may have problems with the *v* sound.

INTRODUCTION

Display a vase. Say: *This is a vase*. Have children repeat the sentence. Explain that a vase can hold flowers and other greenery. Invite each child to hold the vase and repeat the sentence. After all the children have held the vase, say *vase* again, stressing the beginning sound: */v/-/v/-/ās/*. Explain that */v/* is the sound for the letter *v*.

 Invite children to say *vase* in their native language.

Beginning

Part A: Distribute page 69. Direct children to point to the first picture. Read the sentence aloud and have children repeat it. Invite each child to repeat the sentence individually. Then, ask the following questions about the picture:
• *What is the vine in? Point to it.*
• *What is in the vase? Point to it.*

Repeat the sentence, stressing the *v* sound in each word: *The /v/-/v/-/īn/ is in the /v/-/v/-/ās/*. Tell children that *vine* and *vase* both have the */v/* sound. Then, explain that the */v/* sound is at the beginning of both words. Point out that the words *vine* and *vase* are in dark print. Next, point out the capital and lowercase letters. Help children write *V* and *v*.

Part B: Tell children they will circle words that name pictures. Have children point to the vase and say the picture name. Then, have children point to the words in dark print in the sentence above. Ask questions that help children circle the word *vase*. Repeat with the picture of the vine. Remind children that the */v/* sound is at the beginning of both words.

Part C: Tell children they will color pictures whose names have the same beginning sound as *vase*. Identify the picture of the van. Have children repeat the word. Say the picture name again, stressing the *v* sound: */v/-/v/-/an/*. Tell children that *van* has the *v* sound and have them color the van. Point out that the */v/* sound is at the beginning of *van*. Repeat the process with the remaining pictures.

Intermediate

Part A: Follow the directions in Part A of the Beginning section, but substitute these questions:
• *What is in the vase?*
• *Where is the vine?*

Part B: Tell children they will circle words that name pictures. Then, help children identify the pictures and words. Remind them that the */v/* sound is at the beginning of both words. Have them complete the section with a partner.

Part C: Tell children they will color pictures whose names have the same beginning sound as *vase*. Identify the picture of the van. Have children repeat the word. Say the picture name again, stressing the *v* sound: */v/-/v/-/an/*. Tell children that *van* has the *v* sound and have them color the van. Point out that the */v/* sound is at the beginning of *van*. Ask children to work with a partner to complete the page.

Advanced

Part A: Distribute page 69. Direct children to point to the first picture. Read the sentence aloud and have children repeat it. Invite children to talk about the picture. Repeat the sentence, stressing the *v* sound in each word: *The /v/-/v/-/īn/ is in the /v/-/v/-/ās/*. Tell children that *vine* and *vase* both have the */v/* sound. Then, explain that the */v/* sound is at the beginning of both words. Point out that the words *vine* and *vase* are in dark print. Next, point out the capital and lowercase letters. Help children write *V* and *v*.

Parts B and C: Read aloud the directions and identify the pictures and words. Have children complete the page independently.

EXTENSION

Invite children to make a *V* vine. Distribute large leaf cutouts and challenge children to draw pictures whose names begin with */v/* on the leaves. Attach the leaves to yarn to make a vine and tape it to a wall.

Letter *v*

A. Look at the picture. Listen to the sentence. Write the letters.

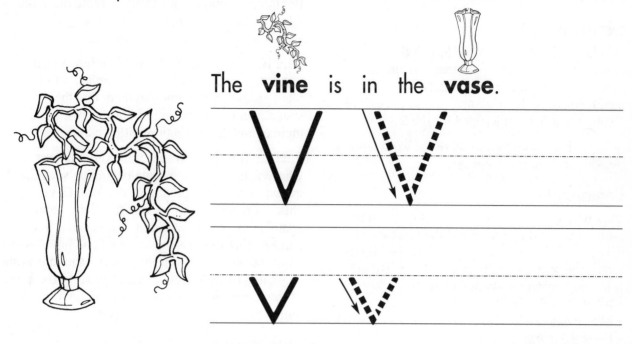

The **vine** is in the **vase**.

B. Circle the word that matches the picture.

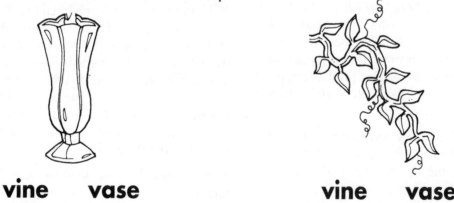

vine   **vase**   **vine**   **vase**

C. Color the pictures that begin like **vase**.

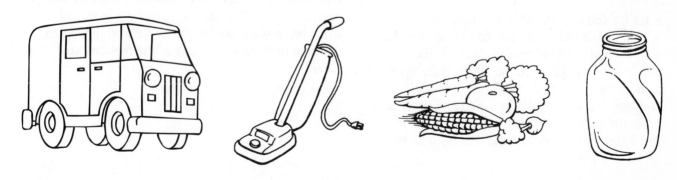

Letter *w*

NOTE: Children whose native language is Greek, Japanese, or Spanish may have problems with the *w* sound.

INTRODUCTION

Display a picture of a worm. Say: *This is a worm.* Have children repeat the sentence. Invite each child to repeat the sentence individually. Say *worm* again, stressing the beginning sound: */w/-/w/-/ûrm/.* Explain that /w/ is the sound for the letter *w*.

 Invite children to share the word *worm* in their native language.

Beginning

Part A: Distribute page 71. Direct children to point to the first picture. Read the sentence aloud and have children repeat it. Invite each child to repeat the sentence individually. Then, ask the following questions about the picture:
• *What does the worm wear? Point to it.*
• *Who wears a wig? Point to it.*
• *Does the worm wear a wig?*
• *Does the cat wear a wig?*

Repeat the sentence, stressing the *w* sound in each word: *The /w/-/w/-/ûrm/ /w/-/w/-/ärz/ a /w/-/w/-/ig/.* Tell children that *worm*, *wears*, and *wig* all have the /w/ sound. Then, explain that the /w/ sound is at the beginning of each word. Point out that the words *worm* and *wig* are in dark print. Next, point out the capital and lowercase letters. Help children write *W* and *w*.

Part B: Tell children they will circle words that name pictures. Have children point to the wig and say the picture name. Then, have children point to the words in dark print in the sentence above. Ask questions that help children circle the word *wig*. Repeat with the picture of the worm. Remind children that the /w/ sound is at the beginning of both words.

Part C: Tell children they will color pictures whose names have the same beginning sound as *worm*. Identify the picture of the web. Have children repeat the word. Say the picture name again, stressing the *w* sound: */w/-/w/-/eb/.* Tell children that *web* has the *w* sound and have them color the web. Point out that the /w/ sound is at the beginning of *web*. Repeat the process with the remaining pictures.

Intermediate

Part A: Follow the directions in Part A of the Beginning section, but substitute these questions:
• *Is the worm wearing a wig or a coat?*
• *Is the wig on a wagon or a worm?*

Part B: Tell children they will circle words that name pictures. Then, help children identify the pictures and words. Remind them that the /w/ sound is at the beginning of both words. Have them complete the section with a partner.

Part C: Tell children they will color pictures whose names have the same beginning sound as *worm*. Identify the picture of the web. Have children repeat the word. Say the picture name again, stressing the *w* sound: */w/-/w/-/eb/.* Tell children that *web* has the *w* sound and have them color the web. Point out that the /w/ sound is at the beginning of *web*. Help children identify the names of the remaining pictures. Ask children to work with a partner to complete the page.

Advanced

Part A: Distribute page 71. Direct children to point to the first picture. Read the sentence aloud and have children repeat it. Invite children to talk about the picture. Repeat the sentence, stressing the *w* sound in each word: *The /w/-/w/-/ûrm/ /w/-/w/-/ärz/ a /w/-/w/-/ig/.* Tell children that *worm, wears,* and *wig* all have the /w/ sound. Then, explain that the /w/ sound is at the beginning of each word. Point out that the words *worm* and *wig* are in dark print. Next, point out the capital and lowercase letters. Help children write *W* and *w*.

Parts B and C: Read aloud the directions and identify the pictures and words. Have children complete the page independently.

EXTENSION

Demonstrate the actions of *walk* and *wave* as you say each word. Tell children that both *walk* and *wave* begin with the /w/ sound. Call on individual children to demonstrate one of the motions you name.

Letter *w*

A. Look at the picture. Listen to the sentence. Write the letters.

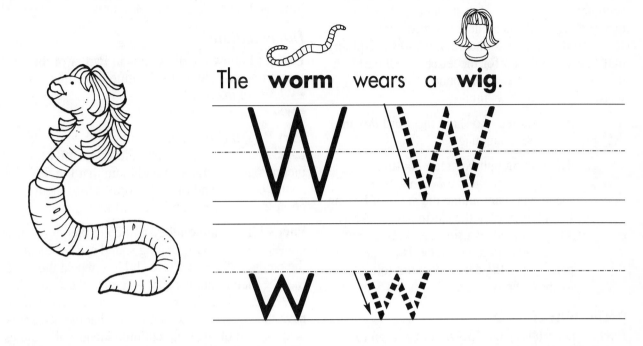

The **worm** wears a **wig**.

B. Circle the word that matches the picture.

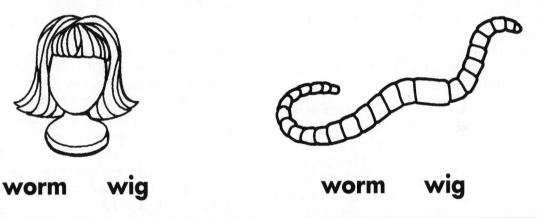

worm   wig   worm   wig

C. Color the pictures that begin like **worm**.

Letter *x*

INTRODUCTION

Display a large empty box. Stand inside the box and say: *I am in a box*. Have students repeat the sentence. Then, invite each student to stand in the box and repeat the sentence. Say *box* again, stressing the ending sound: */bo/-/ks/-/ks/*. Explain that */ks/* is the sound for the letter *x*. Tell children that the */ks/* sound is often found at the end of words.

 Invite students to share the word *box* in their native language.

 The homograph *box* may confuse students. Explain that *box* has two meanings. Pantomime the sport of boxing and then display the cardboard box. Say simple sentences using the word in both ways and encourage students to pantomime the action or point to the box to show the way the word is used.

Beginning

Part A: Distribute page 73. Direct children to point to the first picture. Read the sentence aloud and have children repeat it. Invite each child to repeat the sentence individually. Then, ask the following questions about the picture:
• *Who is in the box? Point to it.*
• *Where is the fox? Point to it.*
• *Is the fox on the box?*
• *Is the fox in the box?*

Repeat the sentence, stressing the *x* sound in each word: *The /fo/-/ks/-/ks/ is in the /bo/-/ks/-/ks/.* Tell children that *fox* and *box* both have the */ks/* sound. Then, explain that the */ks/* sound is at the end of both words. Point out that the words *fox* and *box* are in dark print. Next, point out the capital and lowercase letters. Help children write *X* and *x*.

Part B: Tell children they will circle words that name pictures. Have children point to the box and say the picture name. Then, have children point to the words in dark print in the sentence above. Ask questions that help children circle the word *box*. Repeat with the picture of the fox. Remind children that the */ks/* sound is at the end of both words.

Part C: Tell children they will color pictures whose names have the same ending sound as *box*. Identify the picture of the ox. Have children repeat the word. Say the picture name again, stressing the

x sound: */o/-/ks/-/ks/*. Tell children that *ox* has the *x* sound and have them color the ox. Point out that the */ks/* sound is at the end of *ox*. Repeat the process with the remaining pictures.

Intermediate

Part A: Follow the directions in Part A of the Beginning section, but substitute these questions:
• *Who is in the box?*
• *What is the fox in?*

Part B: Tell children they will circle words that name pictures. Then, help children identify the pictures and words. Remind them that the */ks/* sound is at the end of both words. Have them complete the section with a partner.

Part C: Tell children they will color pictures whose names have the same ending sound as *box*. Identify the picture of the ox. Have children repeat the word. Say the picture name again, stressing the *x* sound: */o/-/ks/-/ks/*. Tell children that *ox* has the *x* sound and have them color the ox. Point out that the */ks/* sound is at the end of *ox*. Help children identify the names of the remaining pictures. Ask children to work with a partner to complete the page.

Advanced

Part A: Distribute page 73. Direct children to point to the first picture. Read the sentence aloud and have children repeat it. Invite children to talk about the picture. Repeat the sentence, stressing the *x* sound in each word: *The /fo/-/ks/-/ks/ is in the /bo/-/ks/-/ks/.* Tell children that *fox* and *box* both have the */ks/* sound. Then, explain that the */ks/* sound is at the end of both words. Point out that the words *fox* and *box* are in dark print. Next, point out the capital and lowercase letters. Help children write *X* and *x*.

Parts B and C: Read aloud the directions and identify the pictures and words. Have children complete the page independently.

EXTENSION

Remind children than *box* and *six* end with */ks/*. Pass out a small box to partners and challenge them to find six of the same item to put in the box. After all pairs have returned, help children to count the items and complete the following sentence frame: *We have six (item's name) in the box.*

Letter *x*

A. Look at the picture. Listen to the sentence. Write the letters.

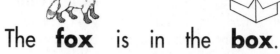 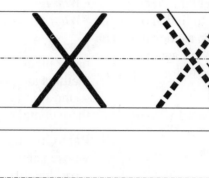

The **fox** is in the **box**.

B. Circle the word that matches the picture.

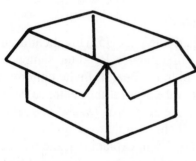   

fox   box   **fox   box**

C. Color the pictures that end like **box**.

   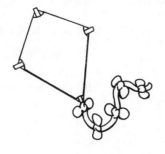      

Letter *y*

NOTE: Children whose native language is Greek, Spanish, or Vietnamese may have problems with the *y* sound.

INTRODUCTION

Cut lengths of different colored yarn. Display a ball of yarn and say: *This is yarn*. Have children repeat the sentence. Distribute one length of yarn to each child and encourage each child to repeat the sentence. Next, invite children to find another person who has the same color yarn as they do. After children have a partner, say *yarn* again, stressing the beginning sound: */y/-/y/-/ärn/*. Explain that /y/ is the sound for the letter *y*.

 Invite students to say the word *yarn* in their native language.

Beginning

Part A: Distribute page 75. Direct children to point to the first picture. Read the sentence aloud and have children repeat it. Invite each child to repeat the sentence individually. Then, ask the following questions about the picture:
• *Who has yarn? Point to it.*
• *What does the yak have? Point to it.*
• *Does the dog have yarn?*
• *Does the yak have yarn?*

Repeat the sentence, stressing the *y* sound in each word: *The /y/-/y/-/ak/ has /y/-/y/-/ärn/*. Tell children that *yak* and *yarn* both have the /y/ sound. Then, explain that the /y/ sound is at the beginning of both words. Point out that the words *yak* and *yarn* are in dark print. Next, point out the capital and lowercase letters. Help children write *Y* and *y*.

Part B: Tell children they will circle words that name pictures. Have children point to the yarn and say the picture name. Then, have children point to the words in dark print in the sentence above. Ask questions that help children circle the word *yarn*. Repeat with the picture of the yak. Remind children that the /y/ sound is at the beginning of both words.

Part C: Tell children they will color pictures whose names have the same beginning sound as *yarn*. Identify the picture of the yard. Have children repeat the word. Say the picture name again, stressing the *y* sound: */y/-/y/-/ärd/*. Tell

children that *yard* has the *y* sound and have them color the yard. Point out that the /y/ sound is at the beginning of *yard*. Repeat the process with the remaining pictures.

Intermediate

Part A: Follow the directions in Part A of the Beginning section, but substitute these questions:
• *Who has yarn?*
• *What does the yak have?*

Part B: Tell children they will circle words that name pictures. Then, help children identify the pictures and words. Remind them that the /y/ sound is at the beginning of both words. Have them complete the section with a partner.

Part C: Tell children they will color pictures whose names have the same beginning sound as *yarn*. Identify the picture of the yard. Have children repeat the word. Say the picture name again, stressing the *y* sound: */y/-/y/-/ärd/*. Tell children that *yard* has the *y* sound and have them color the yard. Point out that the /y/ sound is at the beginning of *yard*. Help children identify the names of the remaining pictures. Ask children to work with a partner to complete the page.

Advanced

Part A: Distribute page 75. Direct children to point to the first picture. Read the sentence aloud and have children repeat it. Invite children to talk about the picture. Repeat the sentence, stressing the *y* sound in each word: *The /y/-/y/-/ak/ has /y/-/y/-/ärn/*. Tell children that *yak* and *yarn* both have the /y/ sound. Then, explain that the /y/ sound is at the beginning of both words. Point out that the words *yak* and *yarn* are in dark print. Next, point out the capital and lowercase letters. Help children write *Y* and *y*.

Parts B and C: Read aloud the directions and identify the pictures and words. Have children complete the page independently.

EXTENSION

Tell children that the color word *yellow* begins like *yarn*. Take children on a walk around the school to find things that are yellow.

Letter y

A. Look at the picture. Listen to the sentence. Write the letters.

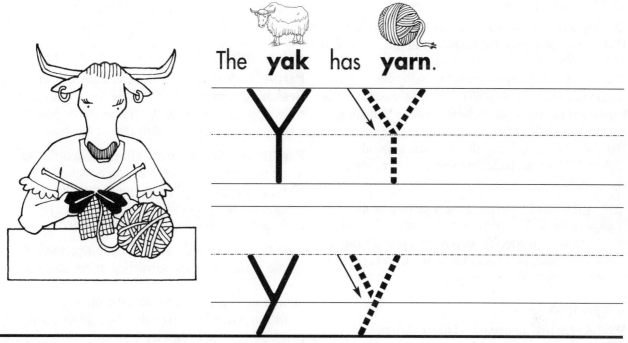

The **yak** has **yarn**.

B. Circle the word that matches the picture.

yak   yarn   yak   yarn

C. Color the pictures that begin like **yarn**.

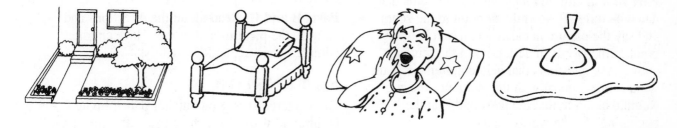

Letter z

NOTE: Children whose native language is Chinese, Greek, or Spanish may have problems with the *z* sound.

INTRODUCTION

Display a picture of a zebra. Say: *This is a zebra.* Have children repeat the sentence. Invite each child to hold the picture and repeat the sentence individually. Say *zebra* again, stressing the beginning sound: */z/-/z/-/ē-bruh/*. Explain that /z/ is the sound for the letter *z*. Next, explain that some zebras live in a zoo. Have children repeat *zoo*. Say *zoo* again, stressing the beginning sound: */z/-/z/-/o͞o/*. Invite children to name other animals they might see in a zoo.

 Invite children to draw a picture of an animal from their native country that might live in a zoo. Then, have them share the picture, talk about the animal, and say *zoo* in their native language.

Beginning

Part A: Distribute page 77. Direct children to point to the first picture. Read the sentence aloud and have children repeat it. Pass the picture of the zebra to each child and invite each child to repeat the sentence individually. Then, ask the following questions about the picture:
• *Who lives at the zoo? Point to it.*
• *Does the zebra live at the zoo?*
• *Does the zebra live in a car?*

Repeat the sentence, stressing the *z* sound in each word: *The /z/-/z/-/ē-bruh/ lives at the /z/-/z/-/o͞o/.* Tell children that *zebra* and *zoo* both have the /z/ sound. Then, explain that the /z/ sound is at the beginning of both words. Point out that the words *zebra* and *zoo* are in dark print. Next, point out the capital and lowercase letters. Help children write Z and *z*.

Part B: Tell children they will circle words that name pictures. Have children point to the zebra and say the picture name. Then, have children point to the words in dark print in the sentence above. Ask questions that help children circle the word *zebra*. Repeat with the picture of the zoo. Remind children that the /z/ sound is at the beginning of both words.

Part C: Tell children they will color pictures whose names have the same beginning sound as *zoo*. Identify the picture of the zipper. Have

children repeat the word. Say the picture name again, stressing the *z* sound: */z/-/z/-/ip-ûr/*. Tell children that *zipper* has the *z* sound and have them color the zipper. Point out that the /z/ sound is at the beginning of *zipper*. Repeat the process with the remaining pictures.

Intermediate

Part A: Follow the directions in Part A of the Beginning section, but substitute these questions:
• *Does the zebra live at the zoo or in the boat?*
• *Does the zero or the zebra live at the zoo?*

Part B: Tell children they will circle words that name pictures. Then, help children identify the pictures and words. Remind them that the /z/ sound is at the beginning of both words. Have them complete the section with a partner.

Part C: Tell children they will color pictures whose names have the same beginning sound as *zoo*. Identify the picture of the zipper. Have children repeat the word. Say the picture name again, stressing the *z* sound: */z/-/z/-/ip-ûr/*. Tell children that *zipper* has the *z* sound and have them color the zipper. Point out that the /z/ sound is at the beginning of *zipper*. Help children identify the names of the remaining pictures. Ask children to work with a partner to complete the page.

Advanced

Part A: Distribute page 77. Direct children to point to the first picture. Read the sentence aloud and have children repeat it. Invite children to talk about the picture. Repeat the sentence, stressing the *z* sound in each word: *The /z/-/z/-/ē-bruh/ lives at the /z/-/z/-/o͞o/.* Tell children that *zebra* and *zoo* both have the /z/ sound. Then, explain that the /z/ sound is at the beginning of both words. Point out that the words *zebra* and *zoo* are in dark print. Next, point out the capital and lowercase letters. Help children write Z and *z*.

Parts B and C: Read aloud the directions and identify the pictures and words. Have children complete the page independently.

EXTENSION

Draw a large zigzag on butcher paper. Invite children to walk along the zigzag after they name a word that begins with the /z/ sound.

Letter z

A. Look at the picture. Listen to the sentence. Write the letters.

The **zebra** lives at the **zoo**.

Z Z

Z Z

B. Circle the word that matches the picture.

zebra   **zoo**   **zebra**   **zoo**

C. Color the pictures that begin like **zoo**.

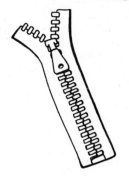 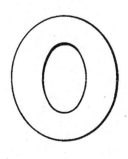  

ABC Order

INTRODUCTION

Review the letters of the alphabet. Then, teach children the "Alphabet Song." Repeat it several times. Tell children that they are saying the letters in the English alphabet.

 Invite children to write and say the letters of the alphabet of their native language.

Beginning

Part A: Distribute page 79. Direct children to point to the alphabet in Part A. Slowly sing the "Alphabet Song" and have children point to each letter. Repeat the process and encourage children to sing along with the song. Then, ask the following questions about the letters:
* *The letter* a *is the first letter of the alphabet. Where is the letter* a*? Point to it.*
* *The letter* z *is the last letter of the alphabet. Where is the letter* z*? Point to it.*

Explain to children that there are capital and lowercase letters. Point out that the letters in Part A are the lowercase letters. Have children trace the letters.

Part B: Tell children they will write the missing letters of the alphabet. Have children point to each letter as you say the letter name. When you get to the space of a missing letter, tell children the name of the missing letter. Ask questions that help them find the letter in Part A. Model how to write the letter on the board as you repeat the name. Then, direct children to write the letter in the space. Repeat the process with the other missing letters.

Part C: Make a transparency of the page. Display the page on an overhead and tell children they will draw lines to show the letters in ABC order. Then, point to the letter *a*, say its name, and have children repeat it. Repeat the process with the letter *b*. Draw a line between the two letters. Continue naming each letter and leading children to draw lines to complete the picture of the wagon.

Intermediate

Part A: Follow the directions in Part A of the Beginning section.

Part B: Follow the directions in Part B of the Beginning section.

Part C: Make a transparency of the page. Display the page on an overhead and tell children they will draw lines to show the letters in ABC order. Then, point to the letter *a*, say its name, and have children repeat it. Repeat the process with the letter *b*. Model how to draw a line between the two letters. Explain that children can use the alphabet in Part A to work with a partner to complete the page.

Advanced

Part A: Distribute page 79. Direct children to point to the alphabet in Part A. Then, invite children to sing the "Alphabet Song" with you as they point to each letter. Next, call out letter names and have children point to the letter.

Parts B and C: Read aloud the directions and have children complete the page independently. Tell them to refer to Part A if they need help remembering the letter order.

EXTENSION

Prepare cards with individual capital and lowercase letters written on them. Pass out the cards with the lowercase letters to children so that all the cards are distributed. Some children may have several cards. Then, hold up a card with a capital letter and say its name. The child with the partner letter holds up the card and repeats the letter name. Give the card to the child. Continue until all cards are matched. Finally, guide children to lay the cards in ABC order.

ABC Order

A. Look at the letters.

a b c d e f g h i j k l m n o

p q r s t u v w x y z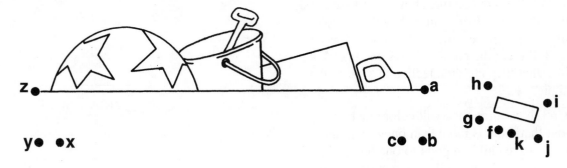

B. Write the missing letters.

___ ___ ___

a b ___ d e f g ___ i j k l ___ n o

___ ___ ___

___ q r ___ t u v ___ x y z

C. Draw lines to show **abc** order.

z •_____• a

y• •x

c• •b

h•

g•   •i

f• •k •j

d•   •e

m•   •l

u   t   s
w• v• •   •   •

r• p
q• o• •n

Number 1

INTRODUCTION

Fill a box with one each of different kinds of school tools, such as one pencil, one crayon, and so on. Write the numeral *1* on each side of the box. Display the box and explain to children that the box has school tools inside. Choose a volunteer and say: *Please find all of the [pencils].* After the child pulls out the one pencil, hold up the pencil and tell children there is one pencil in the box. Say *one* again and have children repeat the word. Continue the process until the box is empty. Point out the numeral *1* on the box. Review each tool by holding it up and asking how many [pencils] were in the box. Tell children they will learn about the number one.

 Invite children to say *one* in their native language.

Beginning

Part A: Distribute page 81. Direct children to point to the picture of the fox in Part A. Tell children there is one fox in the box. Say *one* again and have children repeat it. Invite children to point to the fox and then the box and count aloud with you. Ask the following questions about the picture:
• *Is there one fox?*
• *Is there one box?*

Model how to write *1* and *one* on the board. Distinguish the difference between the number and the word name. Help children write *1* and *one*. Then, invite children to tap a pencil on the desk one time and count the taps with you.

Part B: Tell children they will color the picture that shows one fox. Have children point to the first picture. Tell them the picture shows two foxes. Ask questions that help them realize they do not color two foxes. Then, have children point to the second picture. Tell them the picture shows one fox. Ask questions that help children realize they color the second picture.

Part C: Tell children they will color one box. Point out that there is more than one box in the row. Then, have children point to one box and ask them to color it. Point out that the children have colored one box. Ask them to point to the box and count it aloud with you. Invite individual children to repeat the process.

Intermediate

Part A: Follow the directions in Part A of the Beginning section, but substitute these questions:
• *Do you see one or five foxes?*
• *Do you see one or three boxes?*

Part B: Tell children they will color the picture that shows one fox. Have children point to the first picture. Encourage children to count the foxes out loud with you. Repeat with the second picture. Pause to let children color the correct picture.

Part C: Tell children they will color one box. Point out that there is more than one box in the row. Then, pause to let children color one box. Ask them to point to the box and count aloud with you.

Advanced

Part A: Distribute page 81. Direct children to point to the picture of the fox in Part A. Invite them to talk about the items they see one of in the picture. Have children count each fox and box. Then, model how to write *1* and *one* on the board. Distinguish the difference between the number and the word name. Have children write *1* and *one*. Next, invite children to tap a pencil on the desk one time and count the taps with you.

Parts B and C: Read aloud the directions and identify the pictures. Have children complete the page independently.

EXTENSION

Teach children the rhyme "Hickory Dickory Dock." Invite volunteers to act out the rhyme. Then, help children find the numeral *1* on the clock.

Number *1*

A. Look at the picture. Write the number. Write the word.

1   one

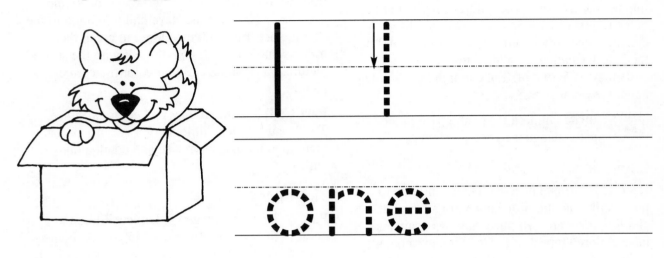

B. Color the picture that shows **1**.

C. Color **one**.

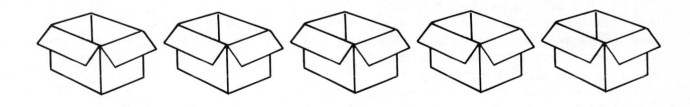

Number 2

INTRODUCTION

Hold up your hands. Say: *I have two hands—one, two*. Ask children to show their hands and invite individual children to count their hands. Next, display a pair of mittens. Identify the mittens and lead children in a discussion telling when they might wear mittens. Ask children why mittens come in sets of two. Say *two* again and have children repeat the word. Write the numeral *2* on the board. Challenge children to name other body parts they have two of. Tell children they will learn about the number two.

 Invite children to count to two in their native language.

Beginning

Part A: Distribute page 83. Direct children to point to the picture of the mice in Part A. Tell children there are two mice. Say *two* again and have children repeat it. Invite children to point to each mouse and count aloud with you. Ask the following questions about the picture:
• *Is there one mouse?*
• *Are there two mice?*

Model how to write *2* and *two* on the board. Distinguish the difference between the number and the word name. Help children write *2* and *two*. Then, invite children to clap two times and count the claps with you.

Part B: Tell children they will color the picture that shows two mittens. Have children point to the first picture. Tell them the picture shows two mittens and encourage children to count the mittens with you. Ask questions that help them realize they color these two mittens. Then, have children point to the second picture and encourage children to count the mitten with you. Tell them the picture shows one mitten. Ask questions that help children realize they do not color one mitten.

Part C: Tell children they will color two mice. Have children point to one mouse and ask them to color it. Then, ask children to point to and color another mouse. Point out that the children have colored two mice. Ask them to point to each mouse and count aloud with you. Invite individual children to repeat the process.

Intermediate

Part A: Follow the directions in Part A of the Beginning section, but substitute these questions:
• *Do you see one or two mice?*
• *Does each mouse wear one or two mittens?*

Part B: Tell children they will color the picture that shows two mittens. Have children point to the first picture. Encourage children to count the mittens out loud with you. Repeat with the second picture. Pause to let children color the correct picture.

Part C: Tell children they will color two mice. Then, pause to let children color two mice. Ask them to point to each mouse and count aloud with you.

Advanced

Part A: Distribute page 83. Direct children to point to the picture of the mice in Part A. Invite them to talk about the items they see two of in the picture. Have children point to each mouse and count aloud with you. Model how to write *2* and *two* on the board. Distinguish the difference between the number and the word name. Have children write *2* and *two*. Then, invite children to clap two times and count the claps with you.

Parts B and C: Read aloud the directions and identify the pictures. Have children complete the page independently.

EXTENSION

Challenge children to name other body parts they have two of. Have them point to and count the parts together.

Number 2

A. Look at the picture. Write the number. Write the word.

2   two

B. Color the picture that shows **2**.

C. Color **two**.

Number 3

INTRODUCTION

Draw an outline of three pigs on the board and explain that the animals are pigs. Point to each pig as you count. Say *three* again and have children repeat the word. Then, explain to children that you are going to tell a story about three pigs. Ask them to raise their hand each time they hear the word *three*. Then, slowly tell the story of *The Three Little Pigs* as you act it out. After the story, number the pig outlines. Circle the numeral *3* and tell children they will learn about the number three.

 Invite children to count to three in their native language.

Beginning

Part A: Distribute page 85. Direct children to point to the picture of the pigs in Part A. Tell children there are three pigs that are wearing wigs. Say *three* again and have children repeat it. Invite children to point to each pig and count aloud with you. Repeat the process with the wigs. Ask the following questions about the picture:
• *Are there two pigs?*
• *Are there three pigs?*
• *Are there three wigs?*

Model how to write *3* and *three* on the board. Distinguish the difference between the number and the word name. Help children write *3* and *three*. Then, invite children to oink like a pig three times and count the oinks with you.

Part B: Tell children they will color the picture that shows three wigs. Have children point to the first picture. Tell them the picture shows two wigs and encourage children to count the wigs with you. Ask questions that help them realize they do not color these wigs. Then, have children point to the second picture. Tell them the picture shows three wigs and encourage children to count the wigs with you. Ask questions that help children realize they color these three wigs.

Part C: Tell children they will color three pigs. Have children point to one pig and ask them to color it. Repeat two more times so that children color three pigs. Point out that the children have colored three pigs. Ask them to point to each pig and count aloud with you. Invite individual children to repeat the process.

Intermediate

Part A: Follow the directions in Part A of the Beginning section, but substitute these questions:
• *Do you see two or three pigs?*
• *How many wigs do you see?*

Part B: Tell children they will color the picture that shows three wigs. Have children point to the first picture. Encourage children to count the wigs out loud with you. Repeat with the second picture. Pause to let children color the correct picture.

Part C: Tell children they will color three pigs. Then, pause to let children color three pigs. Ask them to point to each pig and count out loud with you.

Advanced

Part A: Distribute page 85. Direct children to point to the picture of the pigs in Part A. Invite them to talk about the items they see three of in the picture. Have children point to each pig and count aloud with you. Model how to write *3* and *three* on the board. Distinguish the difference between the number and the word name. Have children write *3* and *three*. Then, invite children to oink like a pig three times and count the oinks with you.

Parts B and C: Read aloud the directions and identify the pictures. Have children complete the page independently.

EXTENSION

Provide stamps or wooden blocks and trays of thick paint. Invite students to stamp three of one item on paper.

Number 3

A. Look at the picture. Write the number. Write the word.

3   three

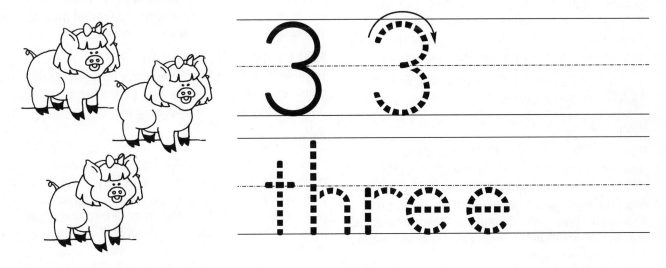

B. Color the picture that shows **3**.

C. Color **three**.

Number 4

INTRODUCTION

Teach children the following rhyme:
1, 2, 3, 4—
Four little birds go out the door.
Then, invite four children to stand in the front of the classroom and point to them as you count. Encourage them to role-play the birds as you repeat the rhyme. Say *four* again and have children repeat the word. Write the numeral *4* on the board. Explain they will learn about the number four.

 Invite children to count to four in their native language.

Beginning

Part A: Distribute page 87. Direct children to point to the picture of the birds in Part A. Tell children there are four birds sitting on the fence. Say *four* again and have children repeat it. Invite children to point to each bird and count aloud with you. Ask the following questions about the picture:
• *Are there two birds?*
• *Are there four birds?*

Model how to write *4* and *four* on the board. Distinguish the difference between the number and the word name. Help children write *4* and *four*. Then, invite children to chirp like a bird four times and count the chirps with you.

Part B: Tell children they will color the picture that shows four birds. Have children point to the first picture. Tell them the picture shows four birds and encourage children to count the birds with you. Ask questions that help them realize they color these birds. Then, have children point to the second picture. Tell them the picture shows three birds and encourage children to count the birds with you. Ask questions that help children realize they do not color these birds.

Part C: Tell children they will color four nests. Explain that a nest is a home for a bird. Then, have children point to one nest and ask them to color it. Repeat three more times so that children color four nests. Point out that the children have colored four nests. Ask them to point to each nest and count aloud with you. Invite individual children to repeat the process.

Intermediate

Part A: Follow the directions in Part A of the Beginning section.

Part B: Tell children they will color the picture that shows four birds. Have children point to the first picture. Encourage children to count the birds out loud with you. Repeat with the second picture. Pause to let children color the correct picture.

Part C: Tell children they will color four nests. Explain that a nest is a home for a bird. Then, pause to let children color four nests. Ask them to point to each nest and count aloud with you.

Advanced

Part A: Distribute page 87. Direct children to point to the picture of the birds in Part A. Invite them to talk about the number of birds in the picture. Have children point to each bird and count aloud with you. Model how to write *4* and *four* on the board. Distinguish the difference between the number and the word name. Have children write *4* and *four*. Then, invite children to chirp like a bird four times and count the chirps with you.

Parts B and C: Read aloud the directions and identify the pictures. Have children complete the page independently.

EXTENSION

Invite children to draw a picture of a group of four animals, such as four sheep or four dogs. Then, help them recite the rhyme learned in the Introduction, substituting their animal name.

Number 4

A. Look at the picture. Write the number. Write the word.

4   four

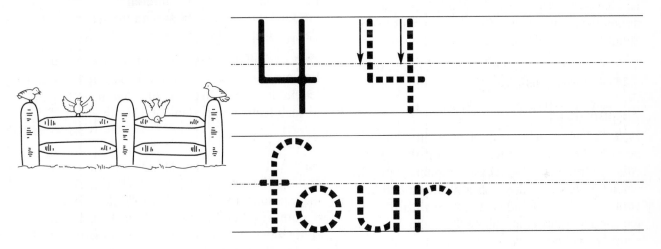

B. Color the picture that shows **4**.

C. Color **four**.

Number 5

INTRODUCTION

Teach children the song "Five Little Ducks." Then, invite five children to stand in the front of the classroom and point to them as you count. Encourage them to role-play the ducks as the remaining children sing the song. Say *five* again and have children repeat the word. Write the numeral 5 on the board. Explain they will learn about the number five.

 Invite children to say *five ducks* in their native language.

Beginning

Part A: Distribute page 89. Direct children to point to the picture of the ducks in Part A. Tell children there are five ducks swimming. Say *five* again and have children repeat it. Invite children to point to each duck and count aloud with you. Ask the following questions about the picture:
• *Are there three ducks?*
• *Are there five ducks?*

Model how to write 5 and *five* on the board. Distinguish the difference between the number and the word name. Help children write 5 and *five*. Then, invite children to quack like a duck five times and count the quacks with you.

Part B: Tell children they will color the picture that shows five ducks. Have children point to the first picture. Tell them the picture shows four ducks and encourage children to count the ducks with you. Ask questions that help them realize they do not color these ducks. Then, have children point to the second picture and encourage children to count the ducks with you. Tell them the picture shows five ducks. Ask questions that help children realize they color these ducks.

Part C: Tell children they will color five feathers. Explain that feathers cover a duck. Then, have children point to one feather and ask them to color it. Repeat four more times so that children color five feathers. Point out that the children have colored five feathers. Ask them to point to each feather and count aloud with you. Invite individual children to repeat the process.

Intermediate

Part A: Follow the directions in Part A of the Beginning section.

Part B: Tell children they will color the picture that shows five ducks. Have children point to the first picture. Encourage children to count the ducks out loud with you. Repeat with the second picture. Pause to let children color the correct picture.

Part C: Tell children they will color five feathers. Explain that feathers cover a duck. Then, pause to let children color five feathers. Ask them to point to each feather and count aloud with you.

Advanced

Part A: Distribute page 89. Direct children to point to the picture of the ducks in Part A. Invite them to talk about the number of ducks in the picture. Have children point to each duck and count aloud with you. Model how to write 5 and *five* on the board. Distinguish the difference between the number and the word name. Have children write 5 and *five*. Then, invite children to quack like a duck five times and count the quacks with you.

Parts B and C: Read aloud the directions and identify the pictures. Have children complete the page independently.

EXTENSION

Hold up a hand and tell children there are five fingers on each hand. Then, point to each finger as you count. Repeat the process and have children join in. Next, invite children to make handprints by dipping one hand in a paint tray and pressing it on paper. When the prints are dry, help children write numbers beside the fingers.

Number 5

A. Look at the picture. Write the number. Write the word.

5   five

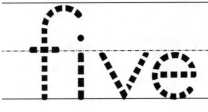

B. Color the picture that shows **5**.

C. Color **five**.

Number 6

INTRODUCTION

Draw an outline of six seals on butcher paper. Say this sentence: *Six seals swim and sun.* Explain that the animals are seals and repeat the sentence. Ask children to chant it with you. Then, point to each seal and count out loud. Say *six* again and have children repeat the word. Write the numeral *6* on the board. Explain they will learn about the number six.

 Invite children to repeat *Six seals swim and sun* in their native language.

Beginning

Part A: Distribute page 91. Direct children to point to the picture of the seals in Part A. Tell children there are six seals swimming. Say *six* again and have children repeat it. Invite children to point to each seal and count aloud with you. Repeat the process with the plants. Ask the following questions about the picture:
• *Are there six seals?*
• *Are there four plants?*

Model how to write *6* and *six* on the board. Distinguish the difference between the number and the word name. Help children write *6* and *six*. Then, invite children to clap six times and count the claps with you.

Part B: Tell children they will color the picture that shows six seals. Have children point to the first picture. Tell them the picture shows six seals and encourage children to count the seals with you. Ask questions that help them realize they color these seals. Then, have children point to the second picture. Tell them the picture shows five seals and encourage children to count the seals with you. Ask questions that help children realize they do not color these seals.

Part C: Tell children they will color six plants. Then, have children point to one plant and ask them to color it. Repeat five more times so that children color six plants. Point out that the children have colored six plants. Ask them to point to each plant and count aloud with you. Invite individual children to repeat the process.

Intermediate

Part A: Follow the directions in Part A of the Beginning section, but substitute these questions:
• *Are there four or six seals?*
• *Are there five or six plants?*

Part B: Tell children they will color the picture that shows six seals. Have children point to the first picture. Encourage children to count the seals out loud with you. Repeat with the second picture. Pause to let children color the correct picture.

Part C: Tell children they will color six plants. Then, pause to let children color six plants. Ask them to point to each plant and count out loud with you.

Advanced

Part A: Distribute page 91. Direct children to point to the picture of the seals in Part A. Invite them to talk about the number of seals in the picture. Have children point to each seal and count aloud with you. Repeat the process with the plants. Model how to write *6* and *six* on the board. Distinguish the difference between the number and the word name. Have children write *6* and *six*. Then, invite children to clap six times and count the claps with you.

Parts B and C: Read aloud the directions and identify the pictures. Have children complete the page independently.

E X T E N S I O N

Invite children to repeat the sentence *Six seals swim and sun.* Point out that most of the words begin with the /s/ sound. Challenge children to think of other things the six seals could do that begin with /s/. Ask them to draw a picture of six seals enjoying the new activity. Then, help children write the corresponding sentence on their drawing.

Number 6

A. Look at the picture. Write the number. Write the word.

6   six

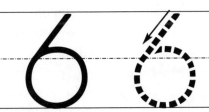

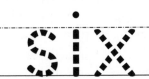

B. Color the picture that shows **6**.

C. Color **six**.

Number 7

INTRODUCTION

Pantomime ice-skating and explain to children what you are doing. Have children share experiences of times they ice-skated or roller-skated. Then, encourage them to pantomime the action with you. Next, invite children to count along with you as you take seven skating steps. Repeat several times and encourage children to join in. Say *seven* again and have children repeat the word. Write the numeral 7 on the board. Explain they will learn about the number seven.

 Invite children to count to seven in their native language.

Beginning

Part A: Distribute page 93. Tell children the animals in Part A are penguins. Direct children to point to the picture of the penguins. Explain that the little circles are snow. Invite children to share experiences of penguins or snow. Tell children there are seven penguins ice-skating. Say *seven* again and have children repeat it. Invite children to point to each penguin and count aloud with you. Ask the following questions about the picture:
• *Are there six penguins?*
• *Are there seven penguins?*

Model how to write 7 and *seven* on the board. Distinguish the difference between the number and the word name. Help children write 7 and *seven*. Then, invite children to take seven ice-skating steps and count the steps with you.

Part B: Tell children they will color the picture that shows seven penguins. Have children point to the first picture. Tell them the picture shows five penguins and encourage children to count the penguins with you. Ask questions that help them realize they do not color these penguins. Then, have children point to the second picture. Tell them the picture shows seven penguins and encourage children to count the penguins with you. Ask questions that help children realize they color these penguins.

Part C: Tell children they will color seven snowflakes. Then, lead children in a discussion of what a snowflake is and where they might see one.

Next, have them point to one snowflake and ask them to color it. Repeat six more times so that children color seven snowflakes. Point out that the children have colored seven snowflakes. Ask them to point to each flake and count aloud with you. Invite individual children to repeat the process.

Intermediate

Part A: Follow the directions in Part A of the Beginning section.

Part B: Tell children they will color the picture that shows seven penguins. Have children point to the first picture. Encourage children to count the penguins out loud with you. Repeat with the second picture. Pause to let children color the correct picture.

Part C: Tell children they will color seven snowflakes. Then, pause to let children color seven snowflakes. Ask them to point to each flake and count aloud with you.

Advanced

Part A: Distribute page 93. Tell children the animals in Part A are penguins. Direct children to point to the picture of the penguins. Explain that the little circles are snow. Invite children to share experiences of penguins or snow. Invite them to talk about the number of penguins in the picture. Have children point to each penguin and count aloud with you. Model how to write 7 and *seven* on the board. Distinguish the difference between the number and the word name. Have children write 7 and *seven*. Then, invite children to take seven ice-skating steps and count the steps with you.

Parts B and C: Read aloud the directions and identify the pictures. Have children complete the page independently.

EXTENSION

Tell children that *skating* names a way to move. Invite children to name and demonstrate other movements, such as running and hopping. As each action is named, lead children in completing the movement seven times.

Number 7

A. Look at the picture. Write the number. Write the word.

7   seven

B. Color the picture that shows **7**.

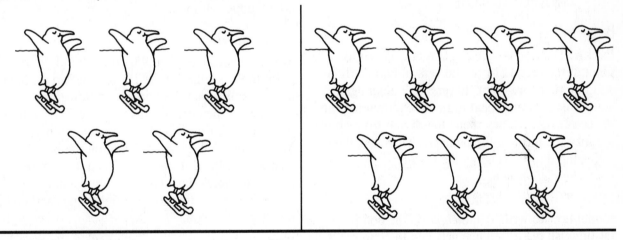

C. Color **seven**.

Number 8

INTRODUCTION

Invite children to draw a picture of a flower. Then, invite eight children to stand in front of the class holding their drawings. Next, teach children this chant:

1, 2, 3, 4, 5, 6, 7, 8—
Don't you think these flowers look great!
Have children hold up their flowers as you point to and count each flower. Invite children to chant the rhyme with you. Next, say *eight* again and have children repeat the word. Write the numeral *8* on the board. Explain they will learn about the number eight.

 Invite children to count to eight in their native language.

 The homographs *eight* and *ate* may confuse students. Explain that the words sound alike, but they have different meanings and spellings. Pantomime eating and then write the number *8*. Say simple sentences using the word in both ways and encourage students to pantomime the action or point to the numeral to show the way the word is used.

Beginning

Part A: Distribute page 95. Direct children to point to the picture of the flowers in Part A. Tell children there are eight flowers. Say *eight* again and have children repeat it. Invite children to point to each flower as they recite the rhyme from above. Identify the girl and the butterfly. Then, ask the following questions about the picture:
• *Are there eight butterflies?*
• *Are there eight flowers?*

Model how to write *8* and *eight* on the board. Distinguish the difference between the number and the word name. Help children write *8* and *eight*. Then, invite children to clap eight times and count the claps with you.

Part B: Tell children they will color the picture that shows eight flowers. Have children point to the first picture. Tell them the picture shows eight flowers and encourage children to count the flowers with you. Ask questions that help them realize they color these flowers. Then, have children point to the second picture. Tell them the picture shows seven flowers and encourage children to count the flowers with you. Ask

questions that help children realize they do not color these flowers.

Part C: Tell children they will color eight butterflies. Then, have them point to one butterfly and ask them to color it. Repeat seven more times so that children color eight butterflies. Point out that the children have colored eight butterflies. Ask them to point to each butterfly and count aloud with you. Invite individual children to repeat the process.

Intermediate

Part A: Follow the directions in Part A of the Beginning section.

Part B: Tell children they will color the picture that shows eight flowers. Have children point to the first picture. Encourage children to count the flowers out loud with you. Repeat with the second picture. Pause to let children color the correct picture.

Part C: Tell children they will color eight butterflies. Then, pause to let children color eight butterflies. Ask them to point to each butterfly and count aloud with you.

Advanced

Part A: Distribute page 95. Direct children to point to the picture of the flowers in Part A. Invite them to talk about the number of flowers in the picture and the other things they see. Have children point to each flower and count aloud with you. Model how to write *8* and *eight* on the board. Distinguish the difference between the number and the word name. Have children write *8* and *eight*. Then, invite children to clap eight times and count the claps with you.

Parts B and C: Read aloud the directions and identify the pictures. Have children complete the page independently.

EXTENSION

Display a colorful picture of a butterfly. Guide children to understand the wings of a butterfly are symmetrical because they have the same colors and pattern on each wing. Next, distribute a large butterfly cutout and eight small circles to each child. Help children count the circles. Then, guide them to arrange four circles on each wing in a pattern.

Number 8

A. Look at the picture. Write the number. Write the word.

8   eight

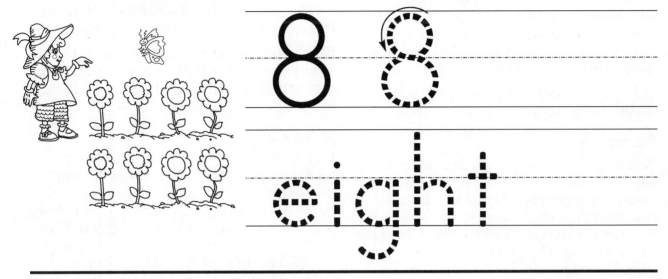

B. Color the picture that shows **8**.

C. Color **eight**.

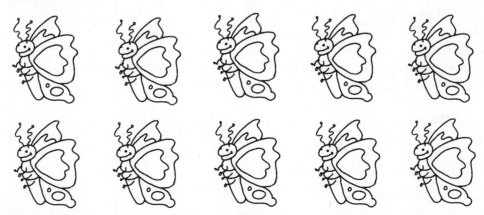

Unit 3: Numbers
ESL K-1, SV 7096-3

Number 9

INTRODUCTION

Display a picture of a bee. Then, teach children the words and actions to the song "I Caught a Little Baby Bumble Bee." Sing the song several times and invite children to join in. Next, tell children that bees live together in a hive. Invite nine children to stand at the front of the classroom and role-play bees in a hive. Count each child and say *nine*. Have children repeat the word. Write the numeral *9* on the board. Explain that children will learn about the number nine.

 Invite children to count to nine in their native language.

Beginning

Part A: Distribute page 97. Direct children to point to the picture of the bees in Part A. Tell children there are nine bees. Say *nine* again and have children repeat it. Invite children to point to each bee as you count. Identify the hive. Then, ask the following questions about the picture:
• *Are there nine bees?*
• *Are there nine hives?*

Model how to write *9* and *nine* on the board. Distinguish the difference between the number and the word name. Help children write *9* and *nine*. Then, invite children to buzz like a bee nine times and count the sounds with you.

Part B: Tell children they will color the picture that shows nine bees. Have children point to the first picture. Tell them the picture shows seven bees and encourage children to count the bees with you. Ask questions that help them realize they do not color these bees. Then, have children point to the second picture. Tell them the picture shows nine bees and encourage children to count the bees with you. Ask questions that help children realize they color these bees.

Part C: Tell children they will color nine hives. Then, have them point to one hive and ask them to color it. Repeat eight more times so that children color nine hives. Point out that the children have colored nine hives. Ask them to point to each hive and count aloud with you. Invite individual children to repeat the process.

Intermediate

Part A: Follow the directions in Part A of the Beginning section.

Part B: Tell children they will color the picture that shows nine bees. Have children point to the first picture. Encourage children to count the bees out loud with you. Repeat with the second picture. Pause to let children color the correct picture.

Part C: Tell children they will color nine hives. Then, pause to let children color nine hives. Ask them to point to each hive and count out loud with you.

Advanced

Part A: Distribute page 97. Direct children to point to the picture of the bees in Part A. Invite them to talk about the number of bees in the picture and the other things they see. Have children point to each bee and count aloud with you. Model how to write *9* and *nine* on the board. Distinguish the difference between the number and the word name. Have children write *9* and *nine*. Then, invite children to buzz like a bee nine times and count the sounds with you.

Parts B and C: Read aloud the directions and identify the pictures. Have children complete the page independently.

EXTENSION

On butcher paper, draw a 3-square by 3-square grid. Number the squares consecutively *1* through *9*. Invite children to take turns tossing a penny onto the grid. Name an action, such as skipping, the child must complete the number of times shown by the numeral on the square in which the penny lands.

Number 9

A. Look at the picture. Write the number. Write the word.

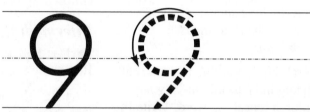

9   nine

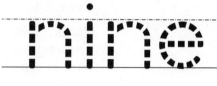

B. Color the picture that shows **9**.

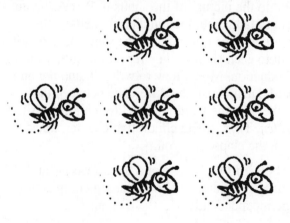

C. Color **nine**.

Number 10

INTRODUCTION

Display a shell and explain what a shell is and where it is found. Then, invite volunteers to help draw ten shells on chart paper. Then, substitute the following words to the tune of "Ten Little Indians."

One little, two little, three little shells,
Four little, five little, six little shells,
Seven little, eight little, nine little shells,
Ten little shells on the sand.

Sing the song several times, pointing to each shell as you count. Invite children to join in. Say *ten* again and have children repeat the word. Write the numeral *10* on the board. Explain that children will learn about the number ten. Save the chart paper for later use.

 Invite children to count to ten in their native language.

Beginning

Part A: Distribute page 99. Direct children to point to the picture of the shells in Part A. Tell children there are ten shells. Say *ten* again and have children repeat it. Invite children to point to each shell as they repeat the song from above. Identify the pail. Then, ask the following questions about the picture:
• *Are there ten pails?*
• *Are there ten shells?*

Model how to write *10* and *ten* on the board. Distinguish the difference between the number and the word name. Help children write *10* and *ten*. Then, invite children to clap ten times and count the claps with you.

Part B: Tell children they will color the picture that shows ten shells. Have children point to the first picture. Tell them the picture shows ten shells and encourage children to count the shells with you. Ask questions that help them realize they color these shells. Then, have children point to the second picture. Tell them the picture shows nine shells and encourage children to count the shells with you. Ask questions that help children realize they do not color these shells.

Part C: Tell children they will color ten pails. Then, have them point to one pail and ask them to color it. Repeat nine more times so that children color ten pails. Point out that the children have colored ten pails. Ask them to point to each pail and count aloud with you. Invite individual children to repeat the process.

Intermediate

Part A: Follow the directions in Part A of the Beginning section.

Part B: Tell children they will color the picture that shows ten shells. Have children point to the first picture. Encourage children to count the shells out loud with you. Repeat with the second picture. Pause to let children color the correct picture.

Part C: Tell children they will color ten pails. Then, pause to let children color ten pails. Ask them to point to each pail and count out loud with you.

Advanced

Part A: Distribute page 99. Direct children to point to the picture of the shells in Part A. Invite them to talk about the number of shells in the picture and the other things they see. Have children point to each shell as they repeat the song from the Introduction. Model how to write *10* and *ten* on the board. Distinguish the difference between the number and the word name. Have children write *10* and *ten*. Then, invite children to clap ten times and count the claps with you.

Parts B and C: Read aloud the directions and identify the pictures. Have children complete the page independently.

EXTENSION

Invite pairs of children to get ten wooden blocks. Challenge them to stack all ten blocks to make a tower without the blocks falling over.

Number 10

A. Look at the picture. Write the number. Write the word.

10   ten

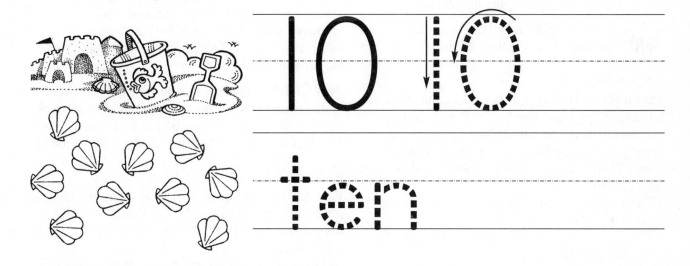

B. Color the picture that shows **10**.

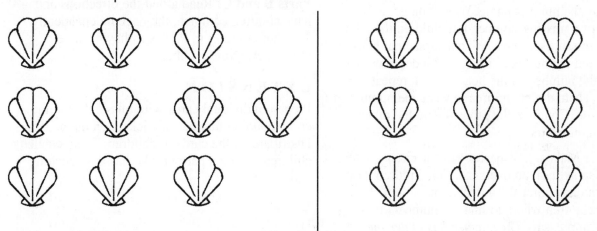

C. Color **ten**.

Numbers *1* to *10*

INTRODUCTION

Display the shells drawn on chart paper completed on page 98. Review numbers one to ten with children by singing the song that accompanies the page. Repeat the song several times and invite children to sing along. Encourage volunteers to point to the shells as they sing the numbers.

 Invite children to write and say the numbers to ten in their native language.

Beginning

Part A: Distribute page 101. Direct children to point to the pigs and numbers in Part A. Slowly say the numbers and have children point to the corresponding pig. Repeat the process several times. Then, ask the following questions about the numbers:

- *The number 1 is the first number. Where is the number 1? Point to it.*
- *The number 10 is the last number. Where is the number 10? Point to it.*

Part B: Tell children they will write missing numbers. Have children point to each number as you say the number name. When you get to the space of a missing number, tell children the name of the missing number. Ask questions that help them find the number in Part A. Model how to write the number on the board as you repeat the name. Then, direct children to write the number in the space. Continue the process with the other missing numbers.

Part C: Make a transparency of the circus picture and display it on an overhead. Tell children they will find and color the numbers one to ten. Then, direct children where to find the numbers in order. For example, say: *The number 1 is under the elephant.* After children color the numeral, have them point to it and repeat the name. Continue the process with the other numerals.

Intermediate

Part A: Follow the directions in Part A of the Beginning section.

Part B: Tell children they will write missing numbers. Have children point to each number as you say the number name. When you get to the space of a missing number, pause and ask questions that help children find the missing number in Part A. Direct children to find and write the missing number.

Part C: Tell children they will find and color the numbers one to ten. Invite pairs of children to work together to find the numerals. Tell them to refer to Part A if they need help remembering the numbers.

Advanced

Part A: Distribute page 101. Direct children to point to the pigs and numbers in Part A. Slowly say the numbers. Have children point to the corresponding pig and repeat the number. Then, call out number names and have children point to the number.

Parts B and C: Read aloud the directions and have children complete the page independently. Tell them to refer to Part A if they need help remembering the numbers.

EXTENSION

Prepare individual cards with numerals and the corresponding number of stickers on them. Distribute all the cards to children. Then, challenge children to find a partner who has the matching card.

Numbers *1 to 10*

A. Look at the pictures and numbers.

1   2   3   4   5

6   7   8   9   10

B. Write the missing numbers.

1 2 ___   4 5 ___   7 ___   9 ___

C. Color the numbers.

Clothes

INTRODUCTION

Gather two each of the following articles of large-sized clothing: shirt, pants, socks, and shoes. Identify each article as it is placed in a box. Have students repeat the names. Next, divide the children into two teams and invite them to participate in a relay. One person from each team puts on all the clothes. They run to a set place and back to their team, where they remove the clothing. The next player repeats the process. The first team to have all players complete the course wins.

 Invite children to share the names of the above clothing in their native language.

Beginning

Part A: Distribute page 103. Direct children to look at the picture of the clothes in Part A. Have children point to each piece of clothing on the clothesline as you say the name. Encourage them to repeat the names. Ask the following questions about the clothes:

- *Where are the pants? socks? shoes? Point to them.*
- *Where is the shirt? skirt? dress? hat? coat? Point to it.*

Next, say the names of clothing and have children point to the ones they are wearing. If other clothing is being worn, identify it and have children repeat the word. Remind them that all these words name kinds of clothes.

Part B: Tell children that they will draw pictures of clothes. Then, have children point to the first square. Read aloud the word *shoes* and point to your shoes. Tell children to draw a picture of their favorite pair of shoes. Pause as children draw shoes. Continue the process with the other three kinds of clothing.

Intermediate

Part A: Follow the directions in Part A of the Beginning section.

Part B: Tell children that they will draw pictures of clothes. Then, have children point to the first square. Read aloud the word *shoes* and ask children to point to this kind of clothing in Part A. Tell children they are to draw a picture of their favorite pair of shoes. Read the remaining words and have children find them in Part A. Then, have children complete the page.

Advanced

Part A: Distribute page 103. Direct children to look at the picture of the clothes in Part A. Have children point to each piece of clothing on the clothesline as you say the name. Invite children to talk about the clothes. Next, say the names of clothing and have children raise their hands if they are wearing that kind of clothing. If other clothing is being worn, identify it and have children repeat the word. Remind them that all these words name kinds of clothes.

Part B: Read aloud the directions and words in the boxes. Then, have children complete the page independently.

EXTENSION

Cut out clothes from catalogs and invite children to sort them into groups. Challenge children to identify the clothing groups.

Name _____ Date _____

Clothes

A. Look at the pictures. Read the words.

shirt pants socks coat dress hat shoes skirt

B. Draw a picture of your favorite kind of clothes.

shoes	shirt
hat	coat

Colors

INTRODUCTION

As you hold up each crayon, sing a revised version of the song "Skip to My Lou." You may wish to sing the first sentence in each line and have children echo it.

A rose is red, a rose is red.
A rose is red, a rose is red.
A rose is red, a rose is red.
Find this crayon and show me!

Repeat with these color sentences: *A fish is orange; The sun is yellow, The grass is green; The sea is blue; A grape is purple; The snow is white; A crow is black.*

 Invite children to share color words in their native language.

 The homograph *color* may confuse children. Explain that *color* has two meanings. Pantomime the action of coloring and then hold up crayons, naming colors. Say simple sentences using the word in both ways and encourage children to pantomime the action or point to a crayon to show the way the word is used.

Beginning

Part A: Distribute page 105. Direct children to look at the picture of the crayons in Part A. Hold up crayons in the order shown on the page and say each color name. Have children repeat the name as they pick up the same crayon. Then, invite children to point to the crayon on the page and color it. Ask the following questions about the pictures:
• *What is a crayon? Show me.*
• *What color is red? blue? orange? white? Show me.*

Next, invite children to sing the song as they hold up the corresponding crayon. Remind them that all these words name colors.

Part B: Tell children they will color the pictures to match the things in the song. Say *rose* and have children point to it. Then, hold up the red crayon as you sing the first verse of the song. Encourage children to join in. Pause to allow children time to color the rose. Repeat the process with each color.

Intermediate

Part A: Follow the directions in Part A of the Beginning section.

Part B: Tell children that they will color the pictures to match the things in the song. Say each picture name and have children point to it and repeat the name. Then, invite children to sing all the verses of the color song. Have children work with a partner to color the items to match ones in the song.

Advanced

Part A: Distribute page 105. Direct children to look at the picture of the crayons in Part A. Hold up crayons in the order shown on the page and say each color name. Have children repeat the name and color the crayon in the picture. Invite children to talk about the colors they see. Next, say the colors and have children raise their hands if they are wearing clothing with that color. Remind them that all these words name colors.

Part B: Read aloud the directions. Repeat the song if necessary. Then, have children complete the page independently.

EXTENSION

Invite children to go on a color scavenger hunt. Assign pairs of children a color. Have them gather items having that color. If possible, award a small prize to the pair that find the most items.

Colors

A. Look at the pictures. Read the words.

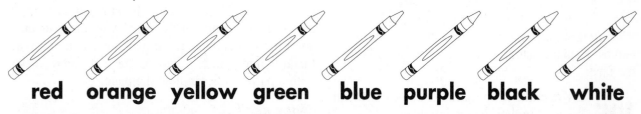

red   orange   yellow   green   blue   purple   black   white

B. Color each picture to match the song.

Face Words

INTRODUCTION

Teach children the song "If You're Happy and You Know It." Incorporate actions related to the parts of the head, such as *pull your ears, brush your hair*, or *blink your eyes*. After the song, point out the different parts and have children repeat the names. Explain that all of the parts are found on the face.

 Invite children to share the names of facial features in their native language.

Beginning

Part A: Distribute page 107. Direct children to look at the pictures of the different parts of the face in Part A. Read the words aloud and have children repeat them as they point to each picture. Ask the following questions about the pictures:
• *Where is the nose? Show me.*
• *Where is the hair? Show me.*
• *Where is the eye? Show me.*
• *Where is the ear? Show me.*
• *Where is the mouth? Show me.*

Review the names of the facial features again, but this time, have children point out the features on themselves. Remind them that all these parts are found on the face.

Part B: Tell children they will cut out words and match them to parts of the face. After children cut apart the words, have them point to the eye in Part A. Tell them to look at each cutout to match it to the word under the eye. Ask questions that help children paste the word *eye* next to its part in Part B. Repeat the process with each word.

Intermediate

Part A: Follow the directions in Part A of the Beginning section.

Part B: Tell children they will cut out words and match them to parts of the face. After children cut apart the words, have them match each cutout to a facial feature name in Part A. Have children work with a partner to complete the page.

Advanced

Part A: Distribute page 107. Direct children to look at the pictures of the different parts of the face in Part A. Read the words aloud and have children repeat them as they point to each picture. Invite children to talk about how they use the different facial features. Next, name different facial features and have children point to that part of their face. Remind them that all these parts are found on the face.

Part B: Read aloud the directions. Ask children if they have questions. Then, have children complete the page independently.

EXTENSION

Invite children to draw a self-portrait. Help them label the facial features.

Face Words

A. Look at the pictures. Read the words.

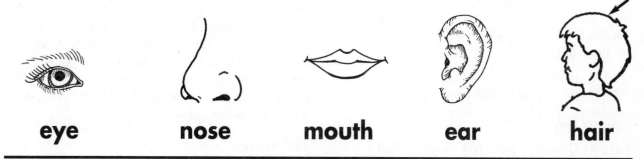

| eye | nose | mouth | ear | hair |

B. Cut out the words. Paste them beside the face part.

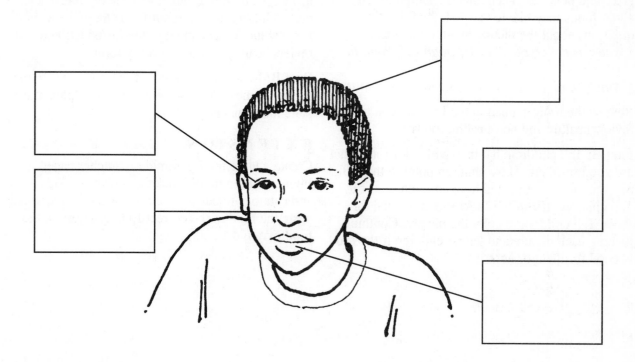

| eye | nose | mouth | ear | hair |

Food

INTRODUCTION

Display different kinds of healthy and non-healthy foods. Name each food and have children repeat the names. Tell children that eating good food helps their body grow. Then, review the names of the foods and have children tell if the food is good for them to eat.

 Invite children to tell about a food from their native country they like to eat.

Beginning

Part A: Distribute page 109. Direct children to look at the picture of the child eating in Part A. Read the sentence aloud and have children repeat it. Tell children that the boy is eating chicken, peas, and potatoes. Then, invite children to tell about foods they like to eat. Ask the following questions about the picture and the sentence:
• *Where is the chicken? peas? potatoes? Point to it/them.*
• *Which word in the sentence is* food*? Point to it.*

Review the foods named in the Introduction to review healthy and non-healthy foods.

Part B: Tell children that they will color foods that are good for them. Have children point to the milk. Say the picture name and have children repeat it. Tell children that milk is a food that is good for them. Tell children to color the picture. Continue naming each picture and telling children if the food is good for them or not.

Intermediate

Part A: Follow the directions in Part A of the Beginning section.

Part B: Tell children that they will color foods that are good for them. Have children point to the milk. Say the picture name and have children repeat it. Ask questions that help children decide if they should color the milk. Pause to allow time for children to color the picture. Repeat the process with the remaining foods.

Advanced

Part A: Distribute page 109. Direct children to look at the picture of the child eating in Part A. Read the sentence aloud and have children repeat it. Invite children to talk about the picture. Then, invite children to tell about foods they like to eat. Review the foods named in the Introduction to review healthy and non-healthy foods.

Part B: Read aloud the directions and identify the picture names. Then, have children complete the page independently.

EXTENSION

Create a large food pyramid on butcher paper. Invite children to look through recycled magazines and catalogs to cut out pictures of food. Help them paste the food in the correct food category in the food pyramid.

Food

A. Look at the picture. Read the sentence.

Eat **food** that is good for you.

B. Color the foods that are good for you.

milk	**meat**	**cake**
apple	**soda**	**vegetables**
gum	**cereal**	**banana**

House

INTRODUCTION

Take children to visit the kitchen in the cafeteria. Say *kitchen* and have children repeat the word. Identify the appliances in the kitchen and pantomime activities that might happen at the appliance, such as cooking. Explain to children that a kitchen is one room in a house. Tell children they will learn about other rooms in a house.

 Invite children to say the names of rooms of a house in their native language.

Beginning

Part A: Distribute page 111. Direct children to point to the picture of a kitchen in Part A. Say *kitchen* and have children repeat it. Invite children to pantomime actions that happen in the kitchen. Repeat with the other rooms shown in Part A. Ask the following questions about the pictures:
- *Which room would you sleep in? Point to it.*
- *Which room would you eat in? Point to it.*
- *Which room would you watch television in? Point to it.*
- *Which room would you wash your face in? Point to it.*

Review the room names and the activities in each.

Part B: Tell children that they will draw lines to match rooms with the things they do in each room. Have children point to the kitchen. Ask them to look on the other side of the page at the actions. Identify each action and ask questions to help children choose the picture of the person cooking. Tell children to draw a line between the kitchen and the person cooking. Continue the process so that children identify a room first and then the action associated with the room.

Intermediate

Part A: Follow the directions in Part A of the Beginning section.

Part B: Tell children that they will draw lines to match rooms with the things they do in each room. Have children point to the kitchen. Ask them to look on the other side of the page at the actions. Identify each action and ask questions to help children choose the picture of the person cooking. Next, identify each room and pause to let children draw a line to the activity that matches.

Advanced

Part A: Distribute page 111. Direct children to look at the different rooms in Part A. Read the picture names and have children repeat them. Invite children to discuss the rooms and the activities that occur in each.

Part B: Read aloud the directions. Identify the rooms and activities. Then, have children complete the page independently.

EXTENSION

Cut out pictures of different kinds of furniture from catalogs. Challenge children to sort the furniture into groups according to which room each piece might be found.

House

A. Look at the pictures. Read the words.

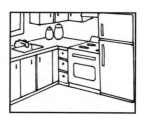

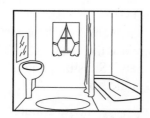

kitchen   **bedroom**   **living room**   **bathroom**

B. Where does it happen? Draw lines.

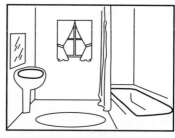

Pets

INTRODUCTION

Display several pictures of pets and identify the animals. Invite children to make the sounds of the animals. Then, tell children that all the animals are pets. Invite children to tell about pets they have. Discuss how pets differ from farm animals. Next, teach children the song "Old MacDonald," but revise the song so that Old MacDonald "has some pets." Substitute the names of the animal pictures in the song.

 Invite children to identify the kind of pet they have or would like to have in their native language.

 The homograph *pet* may confuse children. Explain that *pet* has two meanings. It can be a name for an animal or it can be the movement of the hand as it strokes something. Say simple sentences using the word in both ways and encourage children to raise a hand when the word is used as an animal.

Beginning

Part A: Distribute page 113. Direct children to look at the four pets in Part A. Read each pet name out loud. Have children point to the pet and repeat the name. Ask the following questions about the pictures and words:
• *Which animal can meow? Point to it.*
• *Which animal can bark? Point to it.*
• *Which animal can chirp? Point to it.*
• *Which animal is quiet? Point to it.*

Remind children that pets usually live with people.

Part B: Tell children that they will draw lines to match pets to the place they sleep. Have children point to the picture of the bird. Say *bird* and have children repeat it. Then, identify the name of each place in the right column as children point to it. Ask questions that help children draw a line from the bird to the cage. Repeat the process with each pet.

Intermediate

Part A: Follow the directions in Part A of the Beginning section, but substitute these questions:
• *Does a cat or a dog meow?*
• *Does a fish or a bird chirp?*

Part B: Tell children that they will draw lines to match pets to the place they sleep. Identify the pictures as children point to them. Then, ask questions to guide children to draw a line between the bird and the cage. Have children complete the page with a partner.

Advanced

Part A: Distribute page 113. Direct children to look at the four pets in Part A. Read the pet names aloud and have children repeat them. Invite children to talk about the pets. Remind children that pets usually live with people.

Part B: Read aloud the directions. Ask children if they have questions about any of the pictures. Then, have children complete the page independently.

EXTENSION

Invite children to draw a picture of a pet they have or one they would like to have. Then, have them dictate a sentence about the pet.

Pets

A. Look at the pictures. Read the words.

dog **bird** **cat** **fish**

B. Where does each pet sleep? Draw lines.

 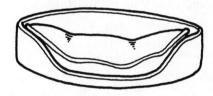

 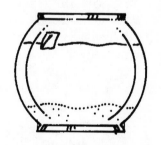

Shapes

INTRODUCTION

Distribute a square, triangle, rectangle, and circle shape block to each child. Hold up a circle and tell children it is a circle. Have children hold up the corresponding shape and repeat the shape name. Repeat with the remaining blocks.

 Invite children to make and identify a shape pattern in their native language.

Beginning

Part A: Distribute page 115. Direct children to look at the shapes in Part A. Hold up a square block, say its name, and have children point to the same shape in Part A. Continue the process until all four shapes are identified. Ask the following questions about the pictures:

• *Which shape is a square? rectangle? circle? triangle? Point to it.*

Remind children that a square, rectangle, circle, and triangle are all shapes.

Part B: Tell children that they will color shapes that are the same. Have children point to the square in the first row. Tell children it is a square and have children repeat the shape name. Have children point to the other shapes in the row as you say the names. Guide children to color the square. Repeat the procedure with the other rows.

Intermediate

Part A: Follow the directions in Part A of the Beginning section.

Part B: Tell children that they will color shapes that are the same. Have children point to the square in the first row. Tell children it is a square and have children repeat the shape name. Tell children to find the shape in the row that is the same. Pause so that children can color their answer. Continue the process by naming the first shape in each row and allowing time for children to color their answer.

Advanced

Part A: Distribute page 115. Direct children to look at the shapes in Part A. Identify each shape name and ask children to find the matching shape block. Invite children to identify characteristics of each shape.

Part B: Read aloud the directions. Ask children if they have any questions. Then, have children complete the page independently.

EXTENSION

Invite children to make patterns with the shape blocks. Have volunteers name the shapes that make each pattern and use additional blocks to extend the pattern.

Shapes

A. Look at the pictures. Read the words.

  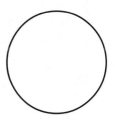 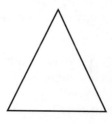

square   **rectangle**   **circle**   **triangle**

B. Color the same shape.

Signs

INTRODUCTION

Take children on a tour of the school to notice signs. Include EXIT signs as well as room signs. Have children say the sign names as well as write or draw the signs they see. After the tour, discuss the signs the children have seen and the importance of signs.

 Invite children to draw a stop sign they might see in their native country.

Beginning

Part A: Distribute page 117. Direct children to look at the picture in Part A. Read the sentence aloud and have children repeat it. Guide children to look at the street sign and identify its meaning. Ask the following questions about the sentence and picture:
• *Does the sign tell people to walk?*
• *Does the sign tell people to stop walking?*
• *Which word in the sentence is* signs*? Point to it.*

Lead children in a discussion of why it is important to obey signs. Conclude by reminding children that following the information on signs keeps people safe.

Part B: Tell children they will draw lines to match signs with their meanings. Have children point to the picture of the bicycle sign. Ask questions that help children understand its meaning and where they might see the sign. Then, read the words in the right column as children point to them. Ask questions that help children draw a line from the "no bicycle" sign to the words *no bicycles*. Repeat the process with each sign.

Intermediate

Part A: Follow the directions in Part A of the Beginning section, but substitute these questions:
• *Does the sign tell people to walk or not to walk?*
• *What does the word in bold print say?*

Part B: Tell children they will draw lines to match signs with their meanings. Have children point to the picture of the bicycle sign. Ask questions that help children understand its meaning and where they might see the sign. Then, read the words in the right column as children point to them. Ask questions that help children draw a line from the "no bicycle" sign to the words *no bicycles*. Identify the remaining signs and have children complete the page with a partner.

Advanced

Part A: Distribute page 117. Direct children to look at the picture in Part A. Read the sentence aloud and have children repeat it. Invite children to discuss the picture and identify the meaning of the street sign. Lead children in a discussion of why it is important to obey signs. Conclude by reminding children that following the information on signs keeps people safe.

Part B: Read aloud the directions. Then, read aloud the words in the right column. Have children complete the page independently.

EXTENSION

Ask children to look around their neighborhood for other signs. Have them draw or write the words. Encourage children to share their signs with the class.

Signs

A. Look at the picture. Read the sentence.

Look for **signs**.

B. What does the sign mean? Draw lines.

stop

walk

hospital

no bicycles

Ways to Move

INTRODUCTION

Have children draw a picture on index cards of how they get to school. Use the cards to create a picture graph. Label the categories and have children repeat the category names. Ask questions about the group to help children understand the data. Tell children they will learn about different ways to move from place to place. Explain that the different ways to move is called *transportation*.

 Invite children to tell about kinds of transportation they used in their native countries.

Beginning

Part A: Distribute page 119. Direct children to look at the picture of the school in Part A. Read the sentence aloud and have children repeat it. Ask the following questions about the sentence and picture:
- *Is a child riding a bike to school? a bus? in a car? walking? Point to it.*
- *Which word in the sentence is* move*? Point to it.*

Remind children that all the ways to move are kinds of transportation.

Part B: Tell children they will group pictures to show the ones that move in the air, on the land, and on the water. Have children cut apart the pictures and spread them out on the desk. Hold up the picture of the airplane. Identify the picture and invite children to find the same picture. Say *airplane* again and have children repeat it. Guide children to understand that the airplane moves in the air. Ask children to find another picture that shows something that might move in the air, too. As children hold up their choices, identify each picture name and have children repeat the name. Guide children to understand why their choices do or do not belong. Continue the process so that children group the vehicles to show movement in the air, on the land, and on the water.

Intermediate

Part A: Follow the directions in Part A of the Beginning section.

Part B: Tell children they will group pictures to tell which ones move in the air, on the land, and on the water. Identify the picture of the airplane. Have children point to the airplane and say the picture name. Repeat the process until all the pictures are named. Then, invite children to cut apart the pictures and work with a partner to sort the vehicles to show movement in the air, on the land, and on the water. Afterwards, lead children in a discussion of their groupings and review the vehicle names.

Advanced

Part A: Distribute page 119. Direct children to look at the picture of the school in Part A. Read the sentence aloud and have children repeat it. Invite children to discuss the picture and the kinds of transportation they see. Remind children that all the ways to move are kinds of transportation.

Part B: Read aloud the directions and identify the names of the vehicles. Have children complete the page independently.

EXTENSION

Lead children in a discussion of rockets, another way to move in the air. Invite children to draw a picture of a rocket they could use to move in space.

Ways to Move

A. Look at the picture. Read the sentence.

We **move** from place to place.

B. Which of these move in the air? Which of these move on land? Which of these move on water? Show the groups.

:ather

INTRODUCTION

Invite children to draw a picture to show the day's weather. As children share their pictures, help them identify the words associated with the weather and write them on the board. Point to them as you say them and have children repeat them.

 Invite children to tell what kind of weather is common in their native countries.

Beginning

Part A: Distribute page 121. Direct children to look at the different kinds of weather in Part A. Have children point to the first picture that shows rain. Say *rain* and have children repeat it. Invite children to share experiences of rainy weather. Repeat the process until all the kinds of weather are named. Then, ask the following questions about the sentence and pictures:

• *Where is the rain? snow? sun? wind? Point to it.*

Challenge children to name other kinds of weather. Write the words on the board and have children repeat them.

Part B: Tell children that they will draw lines to match the weather with the kinds of clothing people wear. Then, identify each kind of weather and clothing. Have children repeat the words. Then, have children point to the rain. Repeat the weather name and have children say it. Guide them to look at the pictures of the different kinds of clothing. Ask questions that help children realize they would wear a raincoat in the rain. Then, direct children to draw a line from the rain to the raincoat. Repeat the process with the remaining weather and clothing.

Intermediate

Part A: Follow the directions in Part A of the Beginning section.

Part B: Tell children that they will draw lines to match the weather with the kinds of clothing people wear. Then, identify each kind of weather and clothing. Have children repeat the words. Have children work with a partner to complete the page.

Advanced

Part A: Distribute page 121. Direct children to look at the different kinds of weather in Part A. Have children point to each picture as you say the weather name. Encourage them to repeat the names. Invite children to share experiences of the different kinds of weather. Challenge children to name other kinds of weather. Write the words on the board and have children repeat them.

Part B: Read aloud the directions and identify the pictures. Have children complete the page independently.

EXTENSION

Track the weather for one week. Discuss the changes the children noticed and how the weather affected their choice of clothing.

Weather

A. Look at the pictures. Read the words.

   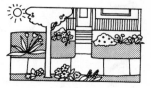

rain   **wind**   **snow**   **sun**

B. What will you wear? Draw lines.

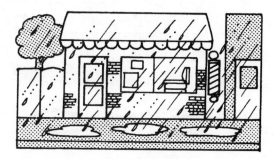 

Dear _____,

You are doing a great job!
Keep up the good work.

_____

Great job, _____!

You know your

_____

_____

On Independence Day, many Americans fly one of these. It shows that they are proud of America. It shows they love their country. When people see this symbol, they stand up. They put their hand over their heart.

4

Diego is holding something special. He does not let it touch the ground. There are laws to protect what he holds.

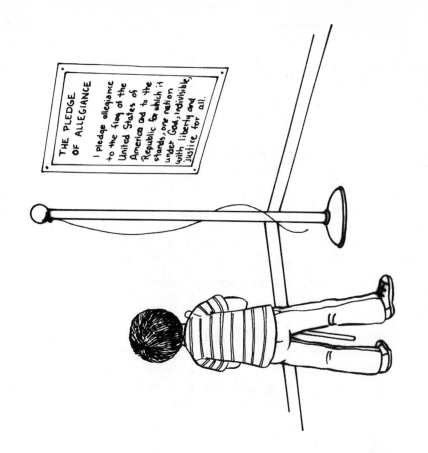

THE PLEDGE
OF ALLEGIANCE

I pledge allegiance to the flag of the United States of America and to the Republic for which it stands, one nation under God, indivisible, with liberty and justice for all.

5

Did you guess what Diego has? Here are some more clues. The President of the United States has one of these, too. It is in the White House where the President lives.

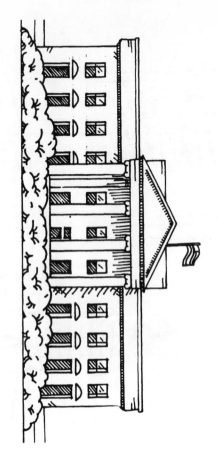

On July 4, 1776, the 13 colonies celebrated. They called it Independence Day. They were free from English rule. So Betsy Ross sewed one of these for the new country. It had 13 stars.

You can find one of these at your school. You can find one of these at the post office and at the library.

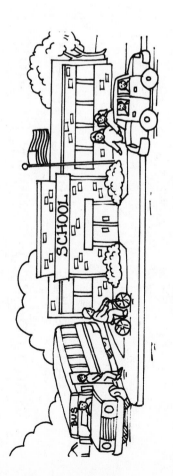

The symbol of our country is red, white, and blue. It has 50 stars. One star stands for each state in our country.

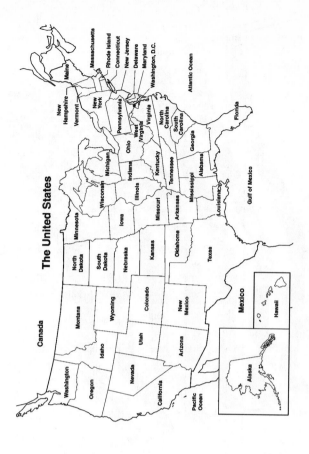

A Symbol of Our Country

Diego is holding something behind his back. It is a symbol of our country. It is a symbol of the United States of America. Can you guess what it is? Here are some clues.

Did you guess what Diego has? Did you guess what the symbol of the United States is? It is the American flag! The flag is a special symbol of our country.

8

ESL Grades K–1

Answer Key

Page 5
Check that children follow the arrows to draw lines left to right.

Page 6
Check that children follow the arrows to draw lines top to bottom.

Page 7
Check that children follow the arrows to draw circles counterclockwise.

Page 8
Children color the three children in a car.

Page 9
Children color the four children outside the shoe.

Page 10
Children color the bee, butterfly, and ladybug.

Page 11
Children paste the fish, seahorse, and octopus in the boxes.

Page 12
1. Children draw lines to match the big cat with the big bed and the little cat with the little bed.
2. Children draw lines to match the big horse with the big barn and the little horse with the little barn.

Page 13
1. Children circle the mouse at the top of the slide and mark an X on the mouse sliding down.
2. Children circle the squirrel up in the air and mark an X on the squirrel whose feet are on the ground.

Page 14
Children color the top chair red, the middle chair blue, and the bottom chair green.

Page 15
Children color the baseballs on the top shelf, the bears on the middle shelf, and the cars on the bottom shelf.

Page 16
1. Children color the "DOG" bowl.
2. Children color the "CAT" bowl.

Page 17
1. Children draw the windows on the house.
2. Children draw the shirt on the bear.

Page 18
1. Children circle the orange.
2. Children circle the shovel.

Page 19
1. Children mark X on the watering, circle planting the seed, and draw a box around the fully-grown plant.
2. Children draw a box around the completed puzzle, circle the closed box, and mark X on the loose puzzle pieces.

Page 20
Children paste the horse, duck, and bird in the round balloons on the left. Children paste the ball, block, and drum in the heart balloons on the right.

Page 21
Check children's work.

Page 22
Check children's work.

Page 23
Check children's work.

Page 24
1. Children draw a line to "listen."
2. Children draw a line to "say."
3. Children draw a line to "raise hand."
4. Children draw a line to "look."

Page 25
Children circle the butterfly, underline the bird, write their name on the tree, and color the sun.

Page 27
B. Children circle: apple, cat.
C. Children color: hat, man, ant.

Page 29
B. Children circle: bus, bee.
C. Children color: bell, bed, box.

Page 31
B. Children circle: cat, cup.
C. Children color: can, comb, car.

Page 33
B. Children circle: dig, duck.
C. Children color: doll, desk, door.

Page 35
B. Children circle: nest, egg.
C. Children color: belt, dress, exit.

Page 37
B. Children circle: fish, four.
C. Children color: feet, fork, fox.

Page 39
B. Children circle: goat, game.
C. Children color: gum, gate, girl.

Page 41
B. Children circle: horse, hat.
C. Children color: hand, hammer, house.

Page 43
B. Children circle: ink, chick.
C. Children color: pig, mitt, inch.

Page 45
B. Children circle: jar, jumps.
C. Children color: jet, jack-in-the-box, jacket.

Page 47
B. Children circle: key, king.
C. Children color: kite, kangaroo, kick.

Page 49
B. Children circle: lamp, lion.
C. Children color: lake, ladder, leg.

Page 51
B. Children circle: milk, mouse.
C. Children color: moon, monkey, mug.

Page 53
B. Children circle: nest, nurse.
C. Children color: nail, net, nose.

Page 55
B. Children circle: olive, frog.
C. Children color: doll, octopus, box.

Page 57
B. Children circle: pail, pig.
C. Children color: pin, purse, piano.

Page 59
B. Children circle: queen, quilt.
C. Children color: quarter, question mark, quack.

Page 61
B. Children circle: rug, rabbit.
C. Children color: ring, rope, rose.

B. Children circle: seal, socks.
C. Children color: sun, saw, sandwich.

Page 65
B. Children circle: tiger, tie.
C. Children color: tape, toe, telephone.

Page 67
B. Children circle: duck, up.
C. Children color: drum, umbrella, gum.

Page 69
B. Children circle: vase, vine.
C. Children color: van, vacuum, vegetables.

Page 71
B. Children circle: wig, worm.
C. Children color: web, wagon, window.

Page 73
B. Children circle: box, fox.
C. Children color: ox, axe, six.

Page 75
B. Children circle: yarn, yak.
C. Children color: yard, yawn, yolk.

Page 77
B. Children circle: zebra, zoo.
C. Children color: zipper, zero, zigzag.

Page 79
B. Children write: c, h, m, p, s, w.
C. Children connect the dots of the lowercase letters of the alphabet to show a wagon.

Page 81
B. Children color the picture of one fox.
C. Children color one box.

Page 83
B. Children color the picture of two mittens.
C. Children color two mice.

Page 85
B. Children color the picture of three wigs.
C. Children color three pigs.

Page 87
B. Children color the picture of four birds.
C. Children color four nests.

Page 89
B. Children color the picture of five ducks.
C. Children color five feathers.

Page 91
B. Children color the picture of six seals.
C. Children color six plants.

Page 93
B. Children color the picture of seven penguins.
C. Children color seven snowflakes.

Page 95
B. Children color the picture of eight flowers.
C. Children color eight butterflies.

Page 97
B. Children color the picture of nine bees.
C. Children color nine hives.

Page 99
B. Children color the picture of ten shells.
C. Children color ten pails.

Page 101
B. Children write 3, 6, 8, 10.
C. Check that children find and color numbers 1 to 10.

Page 103
Check that children draw the correct kind of clothing in each box outline.

Page 105
Check that children color the following:
crow—black
grapes—purple
goldfish—orange
rose—red
grass—green
sun—yellow
ocean wave—blue
snowman—white

Page 107
Check that children paste the correct word beside each face part.

Page 109
Children color the milk, meat, apple, vegetables, cereal, banana.

Page 111
Children draw lines between:
kitchen and person cooking.
bedroom and child sleeping.
living room and people watching television.
bathroom and child washing face.

Page 113
Children draw lines between:
bird and the cage.
fish and bowl.
cat and bed.
dog and doghouse.

Page 115
Row 1: Children color the square.
Row 2: Children color the circle.
Row 3: Children color the triangle.

Page 117
Children draw lines between:
no bicycle and "no bicycles."
hospital sign and "hospital."
stop sign and "stop."
walk sign and "walk."

Page 119
Ways to move in the air: airplane, helicopter.
Ways to move on land: large truck, car, bus, bike, wagon, small truck, van.
Ways to move on water: ship, rowboat, sailboat.

Page 121
Children draw lines between:
rain and raincoat.
wind and sweats.
snow and jacket.
sun and shorts.